preliminary meeting to be held at the Fleece Hotel on Wednesday the 19th November, 1873 at 7.30 p.m."

In attendance were some of the leading professional Gentlemen of St. Helens, including Alderman J. Bishop, Austin Carr, W. R. Thomson, the three Varley brothers, David and William Gamble of the Chemical Works

FOOTBALL.

ST. HELENS v. LIVERPOOL ROYAL INFIRMARY.—The announcement of this match, the first that has ever been played in St. Helens, excepting amongst members of the town club, attracted to the ground a large number of spectators, who evinced a hearty appreciation of the peculiarly characteristic features of the game, their enthusiasm being but very slightly damped by a smart shower of hail. The ball was kicked off at 3-30 by the home team; the strangers, who were several men short, winning the toss, selected the upper goal, and so secured the advantage of playing with the wind. Thus aided, the capital play of their forwards enabled them to keep the ball in rather close proximity to their opponents' goal, and but for the strength of the back players must infallibly have gained some more decided advantage than the four touch-downs they scored by half-time. On ends being changed the aspect of affairs was for a time entirely altered, the ball being carried down into the heart of the "Royals'" territory. This however did not last long, the superior training and backing up of the Liverpool team gaining ground for them in all the scrummages, the excellence of their forward play going far to neutralize the disparity of numbers, as they were able to dispense with all their back players but one, whilst St. Helens had no less than seven. On "no side" being called the Liverpool men had added another touch-down to their score, a very pleasant game thus terminating in a draw in their favour. Where all played so well it is difficult to particularise individual merit, but we would wish to call attention to the rule much neglected by both clubs that, "In the event of any player holding or running with the ball being tackled, and the ball fairly held, he must at once cry down and then put it down," instead of wasting time in mauling, which on Saturday was far too prevalent.

The players for St. Helens were:—

W. D. Herman (captain, three-quarters back)
J. T. Roberts ⎫
R. Thomas ⎬ (backs)
T. Bell ⎭
J. Hammill ⎫
J. Bishop ⎬ (half-backs)
H. Varley ⎭
J. Broome
G. Bushby
J. Forster

D. Gamble
W. Gamble
M. Hammill
E. Jackson
D. E. Jones
J. Pritchard
W. R. Thomson
R. Varley
W. Varley
C. C. Wilson

Match report from the St. Helens Standard — January 31st, 1874.

Chapter 1

The Early Saints (1874 — 1894)

In the Beginning

Ask anyone outside Lancashire what they associate with St. Helens and the chances are they will reply "Rugby League and Glass". This is by no means a coincidental pairing however, as the St. Helens Rugby League Club owes its existence indirectly to the famous glassmaking firm of Pilkington Brothers.

The story begins in the late 1860's. George Pilkington, the Company's Chemist, had left to set up in business on his own and the firm had not been able to find a satisfactory replacement. This was made more difficult because they had set their hearts on employing a German Chemist, as they were considered to be the finest in Europe at that time. In 1870 it was decided to enquire at the Royal College of Chemistry, where George Pilkington himself had been trained. Although not able to come up with the genuine article, the College recommended a young Englishman of German extraction, by the name of William Douglas Herman. He was an outstanding student who, at the age of eighteen, was already making a name for himself in the field of metallurgy. He discovered a new way of estimating the amount of carbon in steel, and his findings were printed in the Journal of the Chemical Society. Pilkingtons were quick to invite him to join the Company, and he took up the post of Chemist at the firm's Crown Glass Works with a starting salary of £150 a year. Before long, the young Herman was travelling northwards to begin a new life amongst the people of St. Helens.

'Herman the German' as he came to be known, soon felt at home in his new surroundings. Yet he missed one aspect of his former life down south. He was a capable sportsman who had played rugby in his school and college days. To his disappointment there was a dearth of winter games in St. Helens. On many a cold winter's afternoon the 'Sporting Chemist' could be seen kicking a rugby ball about with some of his newly found friends on a field near Boundary Road. These young Gentlemen were keen to try their hand at this new game which would fill a gap in their sporting calendar. By 1872 — the second season of the Rugby Union's existence, clubs had been successfully set up in Liverpool, Manchester and Wigan.

It was Herman's dearest wish to establish a rugby club in St. Helens. He looked initially to his workmates, but this came to nothing. Undeterred, his next course of action was to place an advertisement in the St. Helens newspaper calling a meeting at a local hostelry for anyone interested in forming a club:—

"It is proposed to form a football club for St. Helens and neighbourhood. Gentlemen taking an interest in the game are requested to attend a

Foreword

The formation of the St. Helens Rugby Club along with their great rivals St. Helens Recs took place in my father's life time. The support for both Clubs split the town and in that period up to the First World War, as a young boy born in 1902, I can recall a few of those earlier players of that time; Jim Flanagan, Jim Greenwood, Matt Creevey and the great Tom Barton who was one of my boyhood heroes, a family friend and a wonderfully gifted footballer.

In that period after the Great War the crowds and fortunes of both St. Helens' Clubs grew in stature. Before then St. Helens R.F.C. rarely had a team to rival such giants as Wigan; now by a stroke of fate I found myself playing for the club in what was a golden era.

During that period 1925-35 the club enjoyed record success winning the Lancashire Cup and the Championship. It unfortunately never won the Challenge Cup in this era — a bitter disappointment for a team of all stars. The club was blessed in this period with many great players; to select any of this band for special detailed mention would be inappropriate in this short preview, but mention must be made of George Lewis who as well as being a very fine player was an exceptional captain.

On a personal note I am indebted to him for my success for not only did he help me over the early difficult introduction to Rugby League but also, along with those other great players, provided me with those opportunities on the field that helped bring personal success throughout the majority of my career.

For the vast majority of people interested in this history of St. Helens R.F.C. the period in which I played will recall memories of players whom their parents talked about; for myself and those left of my generation it evokes memories of success for the club at a time when the depression was keenly felt in this industrial area of Lancashire.

It is important that a history of this premier club is recorded in detail; Alex Service has spent many patient hours, including obtaining personal interviews, to correctly place in chronological order with the eye witness accounts, the history which created St. Helens R.F.C.'s standing as a great Rugby League Club.

I hope that those who take the time to read this book receive as much pleasure as I did from its contents. For many of the inter-war years the Club became a major point of my life and I still think of the Club, the Town and the players with strong feelings of love and affection which the years have not taken away.

ALF ELLABY

Alf Ellaby (left) shares a toast with his old comrade Jack Arkwright at the Saints' Past Players Dinner, June 1985.

(Photo Courtesy St. Helens Reporter)

Acknowledgements

In writing "Saints in Their Glory" I have fulfilled a long-standing ambition — yet the book would have remained a mere pipe dream but for the invaluable help of a large number of people to whom I express my sincere gratitude:—

The Officials of the St. Helens Club itself, who allowed me to have the fullest possible access to their records; the Staff of the St. Helens Local History Library for their cooperation and provision of valuable archive material; Geoff Pimblett and Members of the Saints Past Players Association for their support, and the recollections of Jack Arkwright, Ted Beesley, Arthur Cross, Alf Ellaby and Fred Roffey.

The following 'Sintelliners' allowed me to record their reminiscences — Ald. W. Burrows O.B.E., J.P., C. Creevey, Minnie Cotton (Thankfully minus umbrella!), 'Owd Tom' Roberts, Mrs. I. Hunter, H. Lowrey, the late Jack Potter, W. Almond and Billy Greenall.

In the search for statistical information I must pay tribute to the late Tom Webb of Oldham, to whom nothing was too much trouble. Two local members of the Rugby League Record Keepers Club also furnished me with valuable statistics — David Hewitt, and the much-harassed Vernon Roby, who can now return to a normal domestic existence!

The writings of several past rugby correspondents have provided me with much inspiration, especially Tom Reynolds ('Premier') of the St. Helens Newspaper and Tom Owen ('Recorder') of the Reporter. Thanks to the staff of the St. Helens Star, including Neil Barker and Alan Whalley, together with Steve Nicholson of the Reporter and Rugby Leaguer.

In addition I would like to acknowledge the help of Gerry Burrows and Ray French of Radio Merseyside; Janice Murray of the St. Helens Museum; the Kirklees Museums Service; T. C. Barker (Faversham); C. Johnstone; M. Flynn (Widnes); T. Auty (Leeds); Mrs. Skepper; T. Delaney (Keighley); Sue Collins; L. M. Donald of Pilkington Brothers; G. Morrison; C. Potter, B. Wilson (Hawthorne, California); Mrs. Kimberley and Mrs. Donaldson for the typing; Steve Llewellyn for the proof reading; R. Jackson who designed the front cover; Alf Ellaby, a true gentleman, for the foreword. A special mention to my teaching colleagues at Grange Park High School for their enthusiasm and interest, and last, but by no means least to Judith, for her understanding and valuable assistance in her co-opted role as 'Technical Director'!

ALEX SERVICE
October, 1985

Contents

Chapter		Page
	Acknowledgements	
	Foreword	
1.	The Early Saints 1874-1894	1
2.	The Rebel Saints 1895-1901	16
3.	The Yo-Yo Saints 1902-1906	39
4.	The Colonial Saints 1907-1914	51
5.	The Great St. Helens Team 1915-1918	72
6.	Turmoil and Recovery 1919-1925	80
7.	Rugby Mad In The Roaring Twenties 1926-1929	95
8.	The Team of All The Talents 1930-1932	110
9.	Survival of The Fittest 1933-1939	132
	Statistically Speaking 1895-1939	145

THIS BOOK IS DEDICATED TO THE PLAYERS,
OFFICIALS AND SUPPORTERS OF ONE
OF RUGBY LEAGUE'S GREATEST CLUBS.

© 1985 ALEX SERVICE

ISBN 0 9510937 0 3

Printed and bound in Great Britain

Saints in Their Glory

1874-1939

ALEX SERVICE

Foreword by Alf Ellaby

First Published in Great Britain
by Alex Service,
3 Ritherup Lane, Rainhill, Merseyside L35 4NZ

The Early Saints (1874 – 1894)

family, E. Jackson a doctor at Rainhill Asylum and J. Broome, a leading tailor. Under the Chairmanship of Douglas Herman, a club was formed. They drew up rules, secured the use of the Recreation Cricket Ground at Boundary Road and looked around for fixtures.

By January, 1874 the St. Helens Club had arranged a number of matches against teams mostly from the Liverpool area. A report of the first home match played by the Saints against Liverpool Royal Infirmary appeared in the St. Helens Standard on 31st January.

What a different game it was then — twenty-a-side with thirteen forwards and the only method of scoring by kicks at goal! The try existed, but simply as a means of winning the right to 'try' a kick at goal. It was possible for a team to score a number of tries and convert none, while their opponents might score a single try, convert it and win the match. Although Liverpool Infirmary registered five touchdowns to nil, these were not converted and the game ended in a 'draw in their favour'.

Saints' fixture list for 1875/6 emphasizes the Liverpool connection, with additional trips to Southport, Warrington and Birkenhead. Goals still decided the results of matches, but if the number of goals was equal – or no goals kicked, then the match was won by the majority of tries, a move thoroughly endorsed by the Liverpool Royal Infirmary team!

FIXTURES OF THE ST. HELENS RUGBY CLUB FOR 1875/76

Date		Opponents	Venue
1875			
November	6	Rock Ferry Vipers	St. Helens
	13	West Derby	West Derby
	20	Rock Ferry	St. Helens
	27	Sandringham School	Southport
December	4	Warrington	Warrington
	11	Bootle 2nd XV	St. Helens
	18	Waterloo 2nd XV	Waterloo
	25	Christmas Day	
1876			
January	1	Open Date	
	5	Liverpool Rifle Brigade	Liverpool
	15	Open Date	
	22	Bootle	Bootle
	29	Waterloo 2nd XV	St. Helens
February	5	Warrington	St. Helens
	12	Fair v Dark	St. Helens
	19	Rock Ferry Vipers	Rock Ferry
	26	Bootle 2nd XV	Bootle
March	4	Waterloo	Waterloo
	11	Open Date	
	18	Open Date	
	25	Closing Game	

The Early Saints (1874 — 1894)

Two or three years after Douglas Herman's sporting ambition had been realized, he found that he could no longer play regularly because of the demands of his career. He decided that there was no alternative but to retire from the game he loved. Herman handed the captaincy over to a Frenchman — Monsieur Le Peton, who also worked at the glassworks, and gave the following advice to his former team mates:

> *"It does not really matter whether you win or lose. What does matter is that you play the game and enjoy yourselves".*

Sentiments that still hold true today.

Meanwhile, Herman had become a key man in Pilkingtons' operations, earning over a thousand pounds per year by 1892. He located and supervised the supply of sand, dealt with all kinds of chemical problems and introduced Pilkingtons into business activity on the Continent. One of the few people to remember him is Alderman William Burrows of Thatto Heath, who was an apprentice at Pilkingtons in the early nineteen hundreds.

> *"At Rainford the firm had a sandwash fed by a box run from the sandfields nearby. I repaired these boxes in the wagon shop. Herman devised a way of keeping sand out of the axle boxes of the trucks, using a kind of flap made of felt. He looked very distinguished, dressed in a tweed suit and knicker-bockers, quite small though stockily built. We all thought he was a German!"*

There is nothing to publicly commemorate Herman's name, except the Rugby Club itself, although his son's name is carved in stone on Rainhill War Memorial. He gave his life for Britain in the First World War.

Gentleman v Players

One early rugby personality was William 'Monsey' Parr, who was a member of the YMCA held in the Ragged School near Brook Street, where the lads would practice goalkicking through the trapeze, using a boxing glove for a ball. On Saturday afternoons they used to watch Herman's old team play and occasionally got a kick at the ball. Some became quite proficient, so much so that if the Gentlemen were short, they invited them to play. 'Monsey' and his pals were so keen that they would offer their services to the visitors if the Saints had a full team.

One vacant Saturday, the club offered to play against twenty of these lads 'from the sidelines' a sort of 'Gentlemen v Players' affair. The team of fifteen Gentlemen promised to treat them gently in the scrums and line-outs. Treat them gently indeed! The young lads in their borrowed togs played so well that they won the match comfortably!

'Schoolboy' Rangers of Eccleston

During the late 1870's, the Club left Boundary Road for a new pitch at

The Early Saints (1874 — 1894)

Queens Park, St. Annes, situated just off Prescot Road — between West Park Road and Boundary Road itself. Eager for revenge, the Gentlemen arranged another match against the newcomers. This time it was 15-a-side, but it still made no difference to the result! Thoroughly dejected, the 'Old Originals' decided that the time had come to hang up their boots. Their captain told the astonished newcomers:—

> "Look here, you can play the game a dashed sight better than us. You can use the ground for the remainder of the season and put your own goalposts up when you need them".

At a meeting held shortly after, above a café in Arthur Street — off Liverpool Road, the new team called themselves the Eccleston Rangers and Dick Prescott, later to become Town Clerk, was appointed Secretary. Nicknamed the 'Schoolboys' they got a few matches to finish the season with Widnes, Runcorn, Failsworth and Warrington.

During the summer months they did their best to raise some cash but were largely unsuccessful. Their poverty was such that Mr. Foster, the owner of the Queens Park pitch, refused to let the ground to them for the forthcoming season and Dick Prescott faced the prospect of cancelling fixtures he had worked so hard to obtain. Out of desperation, he wrote to Lord Derby explaining their plight. Much to everyone's delight — he sent a cheque for five guineas. The money arrived on the Friday before their opening game of the season against Widnes. Up to Friday teatime they still had no field. Prescott and several others approached Ralph Smith who farmed land between Boundary Road and the Clough, a brook long since covered over. He agreed to let them a field where Harris Street and Lingholme Road are now built on.

Would they get the pitch ready in time?

Jim Webb — an original 'Ranger' — described the feverish activity which followed:—

> "Bill Heaton a son of John Heaton — Contractor — also one of the lads, borrowed (I am afraid without permission) picks, spades and handcarts and away we went to St. Annes to dig up the goal posts and get possession of flag staffs and flags, being stopped on the way several times by the Police. Heaton also sent his brother for pegs and string. Others were sent to beg, borrow or steal candles. We struck out the ground, dug touch lines, fixed up goal posts, all by candlelight; working until about 5 a.m. Most of us then went to work at 6 a.m. We played Widnes in the afternoon and won".

They dressed in the open at the gable end of an old barn that backed on to Dentons Green. Ralph Smith took pity on his 'schoolboy' tenants after one particularly muddy encounter, and allowed them to dress in a part of his barn. The ball would often 'give out' during a match and that was that, game over. They could not afford a pump, and Dick Prescott used to take it to

Pilkingtons where Douglas Herman was only too pleased to blow it up for them!

Although results were good in that first season, lack of money was still a problem. They took caps round, but met with a poor response. In those days, the captains decided the duration of the game and, more often than not, it was usually governed by the train service most suitable to the visiting team. When going away the Rangers were never short of players, but occasionally had to make a collection at the station to enable them to take a team. No one could fault their enthusiasm however. Before one game at Birkenhead, Jim Webb missed his connection at St. Helens. Seeing the train go out he jumped down on to the track, ran after it to the junction, caught up with the party and played in the match!

Nomadic Rangers of St. Helens

It was not long before Ralph Smith sold his field for building purposes and the Rangers were on the move once more. This time Dick Prescott managed to secure a ground at Windle between the Vicarage and the Cemetery, from a Mr. Littler. They also got permission from John Arkwright, the landlord of the old Abbey Hotel, to use one of his rooms for a dressing room.

In celebration of their improved circumstances, they called themselves the St. Helens Rangers, and decided to charge a penny or two for admission. The players had to turn up half an hour before the game began to take a collection. Not surprisingly, most spectators waited until the boxes had been round before approaching the playing field. Later they decided to make their collections at half time, which meant greatly increased takings!

A New Rival

By the early 1880's the game that had started as a form of exercise for a privileged few, was becoming part of the life of thousands, especially in the North of England. A measure of its increasing popularity in St. Helens came in 1878/9 when Pilkington Brothers formed a rugby team for their employees. The St. Helens Recreation or 'Recs', played at Boundary Road, to the accompaniment of the St. Helens Public Prize Band, on the field vacated by the original Saints several years before. Their first Captain and future President — W. R. Thompson, had been one of the founder members of the old club with Douglas Herman. Yet it was no longer a young Gentleman's game. "Only those as are used to working hard every day can tackle it" — Rangers' stalwart Monsey Parr observed at the time. "Even we working men have to keep ourselves in trim by boxing with the gloves and exercising with the dumb-bells, which we do every Tuesday and Thursday night during the season".

Meanwhile, the Rangers had come to an agreement with the St. Helens Cricket Club for a playing ground on their field off Bishop Road, Dentons

The Early Saints (1874 – 1894)

Green. Matches with Recs were being played there by the 1882/83 season, creating tremendous interest. The old links with the past remained and, in 1885 when the St. Helens Rangers became the St. Helens Rugby Club, Austin C. Carr was elected as their new President. This Gentleman had been another former stalwart of Herman's team.

Recs Reign Supreme

Newspaper coverage of rugby matches in the town grew from a few grudging lines to several generous columns by the end of the 1880's. The Recs were the first to dominate the headlines as one of the county's most powerful teams. Although they did not play in league matches under the newly formed West Lancashire Rugby Union, their fixture list was impressive nonetheless. Top class Yorkshire outfits such as Heckmondwike and Holbeck drew large crowds to Boundary Road. The formidable Recs pack even provided the town with its first England International, Jimmy Pyke, as well as several county representatives.

"Illuminating" Rugby at Dentons Green

Despite the Recs success, in 1888/89 the Saints boasted an impressive list of patrons and vice-presidents. These included the Earl of Derby, the Borough MP, and great industrialists – Sir Joseph Beecham and members of the Pilkington and Gamble families. Such support augured well for the future of the town team, and on a Thursday evening in January, 1889 the club literally emerged from beneath the shadow of its illustrious neighbours.

> **ILLUMINATED FOOTBALL MATCH,**
> On the St. Helens Ground,
> DENTON'S GREEN LANE,
> On THURSDAY EVENING, JANY. 24th, 1889,
>
> ST. HELENS v. WIGAN,
> Kick-off at 7-30 p.m.   (Mr. Slevin's Team).
>
> The Ground will be Illuminated by 14 Well's Patent Lights, and spectators will be able to view the game as if in ordinary daylight. Admission—Grand Stand 1s., Enclosure 6d., Ground 3d., Boys 1d. Ladies to pay. Members free to ground only.

Advert from Newspaper dated 6th September, 1889

St. Helens played Wigan in the town's first ever floodlit match in front of over 7,000 spectators at Dentons Green. The ground was illuminated by twelve Wells Patent Electric Lamps, whilst the entrance to the field was lit up by another two. The fine weather ensured the venture was a complete success. Wigan – assisted by crack county centre Jack Hurst of Leigh, won an exciting match by 2 goals 1 try 3 minors, to 1 goal and 2 minors. Minor points were awarded when a defender was forced into his touch-in-goal.

The Visiting Maoris

There was another treat in store for St. Helens supporters later in the season, with a match against the first ever colonial tourists to visit Britain. The New Zealand Native Football representatives, or Maoris for short, had embarked upon an exhausting touring schedule. When they arrived in St.

The Early Saints (1874 — 1894)

Helens on 14th March, 1889 they had played no less than sixty six matches since the previous October, winning forty two, losing ten and drawing four. The Maori party — including the four Warbrick brothers, were met at the station by the Saints' President Mr. J. P. Mearns, and several Committee members. A stage coach took them to the club headquarters at the Lingholme Hotel, where they stripped in readiness for the game which was to be played at the old ground nearby in Dentons Green. The teams lined up as follows:—

MAORIS: Full-back — McCauseland; three-quarter backs — F. Warbrick, W. Wynyard, D. Gage; half-backs — Ihimaira, Elliot, Wynyard; forwards — Taioroa, G. Wynyard, Ellison, Maynard, Anderson, Williams, Stewart and A. Warbrick.

ST. HELENS: Full-back — J. Allan; three-quarter backs — J. Hurst (Leigh), E. Foreman, T. Sudlow; half-backs — W. Lund, G. Summers; forwards — A. Borthwick (Capt.), J. Graham, J. Basnett, R. Twist, S. Huyton, D. McLaughlan, J. Ellison, J. Dearden and R. Beard.

The forwards were the attackers and had no fixed positions. In scrummages it was a case of first on the scene, first down. The object of each scrum member was to use his weight or skill in dribbling to drive the ball forward, and not to win it for his backs. The Maoris gave the 5,000 crowd an impressive display of their forward power. Ellison registered their first try shortly after half-time, and it was not long before Ihimaira — one of the characters of the side, added a second. This tough little half-back was, according to the St. Helens Lantern "wreathed in a smile of unusual dimensions". Needless to say 'Smiler' became a great favourite with British crowds.

A drop goal by Elliot and a try by Gage further emphasized the visitors superiority before referee Higson ended a fine sporting encounter. He preferred it that way, as it was to be another two years before referees were empowered to send men off the field for misconduct!

Following their success, the Maoris were entertained to dinner at the Fleece Hotel and later attended a performance at the Theatre Royal. It was a welcome relaxation for the party. After all, there were another seven games to go before the curtain finally came down on their marathon adventure.

A Tale of Two Captains

Billy Cross — 'The Great Half-back'

One story concerns Billy Cross, the Saints fly-half who arrived late for the match against the Maoris. He desperately wanted to turn out for the second half, but the visitors objected. They were no fools!

The former Kendal Hornets and Westmoreland County player was in

The Early Saints (1874 – 1894)

superb form and led the St. Helens scoring list in his first season, 1888/89. He was elected captain for the following campaign and soon represented his adopted county, Lancashire and the North of England.

Work was scarce in Kendal and Cross moved to Preston and obtained a job in a tobacco factory. Preston did not have a rugby team at the time and Kendal was too far away. Two of his former team mates, Joe Allan and 'Pasha' Graham – who had got work in St. Helens and played for the Saints, spoke highly of the club and so Cross decided to throw in his lot with them. A permanent move to the town followed when he became landlord of the Duke of Cambridge Hotel in Duke Street, which was to be the club headquarters for a number of years.

St. Helens relied a great deal on their North Country 'nursery' in those days, and the flow of rugby talent from the area showed no signs of drying up. Saints lost to Kendal Hornets in a match at Dentons Green in March, 1889 – despite having six former Kendal men in their ranks! The fixture also provided Billy Cross with his most unusual half-back partner – Frederick Wells, who was a member of the Silver King Company, playing at the Theatre Royal that week. He took the part of a character called 'Cripps' a locksmith. This 'strolling player' had quite a useful game and cries of "well done Cripps" echoed from the theatre buffs in the enclosure. A Middlesex County man, he generally played with the leading club in the town in which the company were settled for the week.

'Monsey' Parr's Ripping Yarn

The Recs' captain was 'Monsey' Parr, the local lad who had played for the Saints in the early part of the decade. He recalled the day Saints went to Warrington and received an unexpected thrashing. The home players wore shirts of butter-rag, so that when they were caught by a St. Helens tackler – the flimsy 'jerseys' would tear and they got clean away. They cost tuppence ha'penny a dozen, and men went about the field chucking fresh ones to the players who had theirs torn off. Although Saints gained ample revenge in the return encounter, the Rugby Union prevented any further attempts to 'rip-off' visiting teams at Wilderspool.

Monsey's team mate and silent partner 'Dummy' Tickle had also played for the Saints in the old days. A dumb mute – the Recs answer to Harpo Marx kept spirits high with his mimicry and antics, holding auction sales and pretending to sing. The two old warhorses spent their last playing days together at Pilkingtons new recreation grounds at City Road, paid for by workers subscriptions, where there was plenty of room for cricket and bowls – as well as football.

The Green Grass of Home

It was just over ninety-five years ago, on Saturday, 6th September, 1890 that the St. Helens club played its first game on the Knowsley Road turf,

The Early Saints (1874 — 1894)

when Manchester Rangers — one of the strongest teams in the North of England — provided the opposition. Compared to their former pitch at Dentons Green, which they had been forced to leave at the end of the previous season, the distance of the new enclosure from the centre of town was considered to be a disadvantage. Despite this, a crowd of between two and three thousand enthusiasts eagerly gathered in the brilliant sunshine.

The Saints, wearing chocolate and sky blue jerseys, lined up in an unusual way. No wonder it was a forwards' game in those days:—

Back — Lomax; threequarters — Sudlow, Foulkes, Unsworth; halves — Cross (Capt.), Little; forwards — Borthwick, Barnes, Gladwin, Basnett, R. Twist, John Brownbill, Joseph Brownbill, Guest and Rankin.

Lt. Colonel Wilcock, Chairman of the St. Helens Committee kicked off and the game soon developed into a fast, exciting affair, and it was not long before the home side opened their account. Saints' captain Billy Cross had the honour of getting the first points, a drop goal after a scrum on the Rangers' twenty five.

St. Helens supporters had even more to cheer about shortly afterwards. Joseph Brownbill caught the ball from a line-out or 'throw-out' as it was then called, and plunged over the line for a try. His brother John failed with the conversion.

Alan Borthwick, the former Eccleston Ranger, made sure of victory with another goal in the second half. The visitors also notched a consolation try to make the final score St. Helens 2 goals 1 try 4 minors, Rangers 1 try 1 minor.

Saints fixture list had an unfamiliar look about it. Clubs such as Askam, Walkden, Blackley, Ulverston, Kendal and Dukinfield provided the opposition, as well as the more familiar names of Wigan, Widnes, Leigh and Oldham.

Today's spectators would find it difficult to imagine the Knowlsey Road Ground in 1890. It was just a field, and the stewards took pay at pigeon holes in the fencing at the Eccleston end. Later, at the town end, they had three or four turnstiles. There is an item 'fencing etc., £100.6s.0d' in the 1890/91 accounts and their rent was £30. Gates were anything from £20 to £40.

How times have changed

NOTICE.

ST. HELENS FOOTBALL CLUB.

THE DISTRIBUTION OF PRIZES, Advertised to take place on March 12th, is POSTPONED until APRIL 20, 1888, in consequence of its clashing with the W.L. Cup Ties, and will positively take place on that day. Prizes to the amount of £120. First Prize 58gs.; Second, £15; Third, £5.

Tickets, 6d. each, may be had from
A. HOUGHTON, Financial Secretary.

Extract from Newspaper dated 6th September, 1889

The Early Saints (1874 — 1894)   11

— on 11th March, 1984 — a near twenty thousand crowd assembled at Knowsley Road for the third round Challenge Cup tie between Saints and Wigan, paying over £36,000 for the privilege.

SHOCKING ACCIDENT IN THE
FOOTBALL FIELD AT ST. HELENS

A serious accident occurred on Saturday afternoon on the Recreation football ground, St. Helens — in a match between St. Helens Recreation Club and the Wigan Club, when the local captain — William Parr, better known among the admirers of football as 'Monsey', received serious injuries. Shortly after the game commenced a scrimmage took place, when Parr either fell or was thrown to the ground, several other players falling upon him. Parr was unable to rise, and although it was first thought he was only 'winded' and would recover in a few minutes, it was soon afterwards seen that he was in an unconscious state. In this condition he was carried to the pavilion where Dr. F. Knowles — who was upon the ground, attended him. So serious did Parr's condition become, he having sustained internal injuries and such a shock as to be in a state of collapse, that he was taken to the Providence Hospital, where an operation was performed by Dr. Knowles. The news spread through the town that death had ensued, but this was promptly contradicted; the fact being that under the skillful treatment of the medical gentleman — consciousness was restored in about an hour after admission, and it is hoped that with a few days rest and care, Parr will be convalescent. An instance of the ruling passion of football enthusiasts was given by Parr who, on recovering consciousness, and without knowing what had happened or where he was, exclaimed — "Who's won?"

PRESCOT REPORTER AND
ST. HELENS CENTRAL ADVERTISER
7th APRIL, 1888

"I'm thirty one years old and not married yet, for what girl 'ud marry such an unlucky beggar as me? You see I keep getting into th'wars" said Monsey Parr just before he finished playing. Looking at this extract we can understand how he must have felt!

There was no love lost between the teams in this match. When the final whistle blew, one spectator had even gone so far as to strike the Wigan captain on the face with a dead rat!

The March Forward

Those supporters who made the 'long walk' to Saints new ground saw their teams fortunes fade somewhat after a promising start. The red-shirted Recs once again grabbed the headlines with some impressive victories against strong Lancashire and Yorkshire combinations. Over 8,000 people packed into the Boundary Road enclosure to watch the 'Good Old Rekerashun' tame the Lions of Swinton. A similar number were present for the Roses battle against Brighouse Rangers.

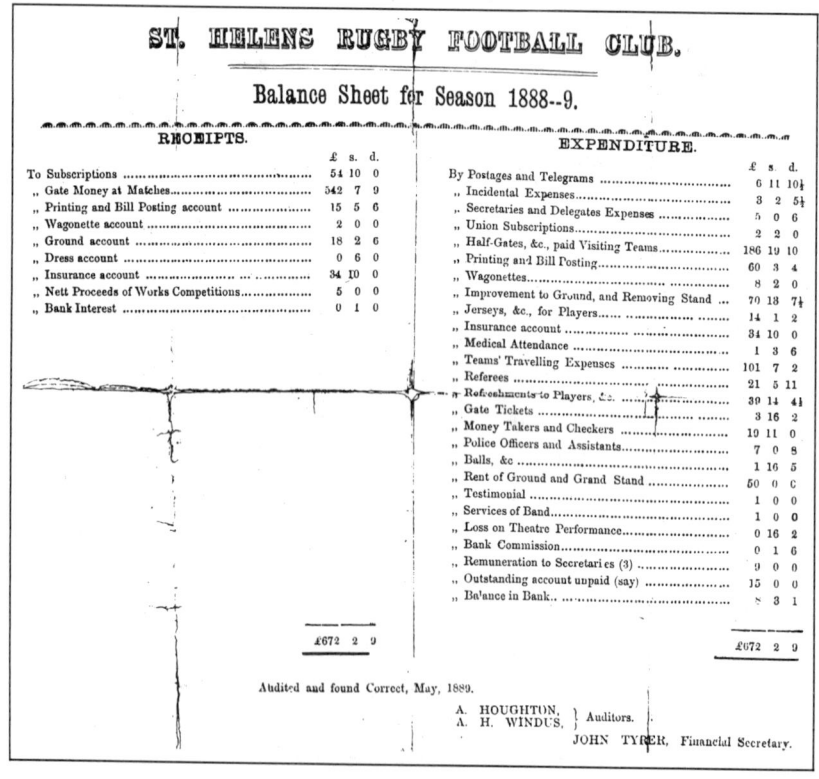

ST. HELENS RUGBY FOOTBALL CLUB.

Balance Sheet for Season 1888--9.

RECEIPTS.	£	s.	d.	EXPENDITURE.	£	s.	d.
To Subscriptions	54	10	0	By Postages and Telegrams	6	11	10½
„ Gate Money at Matches	542	7	9	„ Incidental Expenses	3	2	5¼
„ Printing and Bill Posting account	15	5	6	„ Secretaries and Delegates Expenses	5	0	6
„ Wagonette account	2	0	0	„ Union Subscriptions	2	2	0
„ Ground account	18	2	6	„ Half-Gates, &c., paid Visiting Teams	186	19	10
„ Dress account	0	6	0	„ Printing and Bill Posting	60	3	4
„ Insurance account	34	10	0	„ Wagonettes	8	2	0
„ Nett Proceeds of Works Competitions	5	0	0	„ Improvement to Ground, and Removing Stand	70	18	7¼
„ Bank Interest	0	1	0	„ Jerseys, &c., for Players	14	1	2
				„ Insurance account	34	10	0
				„ Medical Attendance	1	3	6
				„ Teams' Travelling Expenses	101	7	2
				„ Referees	21	5	11
				„ Refreshments to Players, &c.	39	14	4½
				„ Gate Tickets	3	16	2
				„ Money Takers and Checkers	19	11	0
				„ Police Officers and Assistants	7	0	8
				„ Balls, &c	1	16	5
				„ Rent of Ground and Grand Stand	50	0	0
				„ Testimonial	1	0	0
				„ Services of Band	1	0	0
				„ Loss on Theatre Performance	0	16	2
				„ Bank Commission	0	1	6
				„ Remuneration to Secretaries (3)	9	0	0
				„ Outstanding account unpaid (say)	15	0	0
				„ Balance in Bank	8	3	1
	£672	2	9		£672	2	9

Audited and found Correct, May, 1889.

A. HOUGHTON, } Auditors.
A. H. WINDUS, }

JOHN TYRER, Financial Secretary.

(Courtesy Mrs. Skepper)

Despite the presence of such formidable local rivals, the St. Helens club advanced considerably both on and off the field in the early 1890's. A Baronet, two MP's and two JP's appeared among its patrons, while the list of vice-presidents even included a reverend gentleman by the name of Canon Willink. The Committee's faith in Billy Cross — surely one of the earliest examples of a player coach in rugby, was fully justified. Results improved and the club was able to strengthen its fixture list accordingly.

When compiling their list of matches, the Saints officials always tried to avoid clashes with the Recs. The result was improved gates and each club had the chance of catering for the others spectators as well as its own. This 'live and let live' arrangement was shattered with the extension of the

The Early Saints (1874 – 1894)

Lancashire Cup Competition into three divisions in the summer of 1893. The Recs had not entered the competition since the middle eighties, and were to continue with games on a friendly basis only. 'Monsey' Parr explained why in 1889:—

> "Th' masters don't like 'em. After that affair with Widnes two years ago when one young fellow was killed, and another had his leg broken, they said we'd better give up cup ties and such things; and you must do as your masters want or else shut up shop".

ANOTHER PAINFUL FOOTBALL ACCIDENT

> On Saturday during the progress of a rugby football match between St. Helens 'A' and West Leigh, a serious accident happened to Edward Smith, aged 19, of Waterloo Street, St. Helens. Smith was a new player, and had no bars on his shoes, and the result was that he slipped and fell on his head, which was crushed down upon his chest. Paralysis quickly set in, and Dr. Jones was called in and ordered his removal to the Workhouse Hospital, where he lies in a dying condition. He was the only support of his widowed mother.

REPORT IN THE ST. HELENS NEWSPAPER SATURDAY, APRIL 5th, 1890

Meanwhile, St. Helens were selected for the second division and immediately had eighteen Saturdays earmarked for cup matches. When the Saints and Recs fixture cards were compared, it was found that on eight dates both the first teams were out of town, and on nine occasions both first teams were at home, thus dividing spectators and gates. The local press summed up the dilemma as follows:—

> "The second Saturday in September shows that the Swinton Lions will open the Boundary Road ground, whilst Wigan are antagonizing St. Helens at Knowsley Road. It will be difficult to decide which to witness......... on 18th November the game between Recs and Wigan will take all the interest out of Saints match with Tuebrook".

Those 'floating' rugby spectators in St. Helens were definitely spoilt for choice as Recs continued to play some excellent football and the Saints at

St. Helens Rugby Football Club.

SATURDAY, Nov. 18th, 1893.

First Team v. Tuebrook, at St. Helens.

Full Back :—T. Foulkes.
Three Quarter Backs :—R. Doherty, D. Traynor, J. Appleton.
Half Backs :—W. Cross, J. McLees.
Forwards :—J. Brownhill, J. Gladwin, W. Wilson, W. Whiteley, F. Brownbell, T. Winstanley, E. Ashcroft, J. Graham, S. Jones
Reserve—   Umpire—J. Edwards.
Kick-off 3-0   Trainer— J. Gent.

One of the earliest surviving St. Helens teamsheets

Our Football Competition.

Every week during the Football season, commencing to day, we shall give A GUINEA CASH PRIZE to the most successful guesser at the results of certain of the matches fixed to be played on the Saturday of the following week.

Thus, on Saturday, the 14th inst., the following matches, among others which we have not been able to ascertain, will be played :—

Morley v. St. Helens.	St. Helens "Recs." "A" v. Poolstock.
Kirkstall v. St. Helens "Recs."	Aigburth Vale "A" v. St. Helens Asso.
Aigburth Vale v. St. Helens Association.	Warrington v. Swinton
St. Helens "A" v. St. Helens Old Boys.	Globe Recreation v. Wigan "A."
Tyldesley v. Wortley.	

Whoever makes the best guess at the scores of the competing teams named will receive the prize ; and the winning guess or guesses will be published in the issue in which the prize is awarded.

Guesses in the first Competition must be forwarded to the *Lantern* office, on Coupon No. 1 ; not later than Thursday, the 12th inst. The same Competitor may forward any number of guesses so long as each set is on a different Coupon. One Coupon, that is to say, covers one set of guesses as to the results of the whole set of announced matches.

Next week, of course, the Competition will relate to matches of the following week ; and so on throughout the season.

"LANTERN" FOOTBALL COMPETITIONS.

Competition No. 1—Matches of 14th September, 1889.

	G	T	M		G	T	M
Morley				St. Helens			
Kirkstall				St. Helens "Recs."			
St. Helens Association				Aigburth Vale			
St. Helens "A"				St. Helens Old Boys			
St. Helens "Recs." "A"				Poolstock			
Aigburth Vale "A"				St. Helens Association "A"			
Warrington				Swinton			
Tyldesley				Wortley			

Name and Address of Guesser ....

Extract from Newspaper dated 6th September, 1889

The Early Saints (1874 — 1894)

last showed that they were becoming a force to be reckoned with. Not only did they defeat the likes of Swinton, Runcorn, Wigan and Warrington in 'friendly' matches at Knowsley Road, but also ran away with the Second Division Championship.

It seemed fitting after the final match against Tyldesley that the Saints first trophy should be presented to Billy Cross by Mr. Henry Seton-Karr. This well known patron of the club was St. Helens' first ever Member of Parliament, having represented the town since 1885. The magnificent cup with the inscription 'Lancashire County Rugby Challenge Cup 2nd Division — presented by West Lancs and Border Towns Rugby Union, 1894' — and worth in excess of seventy five guineas, was held up by the skipper to the delight of the St. Helens faithful in front of the packed grandstand.

There were individual cheers as each player received his commemorative gold medal from the Borough Member. Not surprisingly, Bob Doherty and Tommy Sudlow received extra special ovations. The two flying wingers had notched up over fifty tries between them during the campaign. In a short speech at the end of the presentations, Mr. Seton-Karr thought it remarkable how rugby football, now no longer just a 'young Gentleman's game — had become so popular in the area:—

"The Duke of Wellington once said that the Battle of Waterloo was won on the playing fields of Eton. That was, of course, when football was largely confined to the public schools. If the Duke had been here today, he would have said that any future battles of Waterloo would be won on the playing fields of St. Helens and Lancashire".

He was not to know that twenty years later those words were to ring true on the battlefields of France.

That night — in response to the kind invitation of Mr. Wallace Revill, the Theatre Royal Manager, the team attended a performance of the drama 'It's Never Too Late To Mend'. They occupied the place of honour in the centre circle, and appeared to greatly enjoy themselves. I wonder whether such after-match entertainment would appeal to the modern-day Saints?

Chapter 2

The Rebel Saints (1895 – 1901)

Northern Union Pioneers

Saints' rugby success came at a time when storm clouds were gathering in the northern industrial towns. Clubs paid expenses to working men who forfeited a Saturday shift to play rugby. Indeed there were many working class players who claimed they could not afford to play unless they were compensated for such lost time. These 'broken time' payments were no more than a few bob, yet ninety years ago that counted for much when a sovereign had to keep many a family for a week.

A clash seemed inevitable, and matters came to a head at the annual meeting of the Rugby Union in London on 20th September, 1893. A proposal by two Yorkshire representatives – J. A. Millar and M. Newsome, that 'players be allowed compensation for bona-fide loss of time' was defeated by 282 votes to 136. The Rugby Union establishment in the South was flatly against any form of compensation, seeing it only as the thin end of the wedge to professionalism.

Despite this, Northern clubs insisted on paying broken time. As the 1894/95 season proceeded, first Leigh (19th Sept.) then Salford (16th Oct.) and Wigan (13th Nov.) were found guilty of alleged professionalism. The Riversiders were suspended until 1st February and, like the two other clubs, struck out of the Cup Competition. Commenting on the proceedings of the Lancashire County Committee, 'Crossbar' in the Wigan Observer wrote:—

> "So Wigan have met their fate. Not that I would say their hands are cleaner than other big Lancashire clubs – they are all more or less tarred with the same brush ..... of course it is not safe to prophesy but, nevertheless, there is a general disposition in the North to form a separatist body from the Rugby Union".

The die was cast on 29th August, 1895 when the representatives of twenty one of the principal rugby clubs in the North of England met at the George Hotel in Huddersfield and duly resigned from the Rugby Union. The meeting lasted three hours, and the following clubs were represented:

Brighouse Rangers, Rochdale Hornets, Halifax, Leeds, Manningham, Bradford, Hull, Huddersfield, Hunslet, Wakefield, Liversedge, Dewsbury, Batley, Oldham, Broughton Rangers, St. Helens, Leigh, Warrington, Tyldesley, Wigan and Widnes.

Secretary Fred Dennet represented the Saints. After full discussion, the following resolution had been adopted:—

> "That the Clubs represented decide to form a Northern Rugby Football

The Rebel Saints (1895 — 1901)

Union, and pledge themselves to push forward, without delay, its establishment on the principle of payment for bona-fide time only".

Six shillings broken time payment per day was the originally stipulated figure at the birth of the new Union, although it was not long before the wealthier and more successful clubs began to pay more inflated amounts. The Rugby Union's reaction was to forbid its member clubs to play matches against the Northern Union rebels, who now numbered twenty two with the withdrawal of Dewsbury and the addition of Stockport and Runcorn. 'Spectator' in The St. Helens Newspaper, mirrored the spirit of optimism shown by Saints enthusiasts in the town:—

> "The Committee of the St. Helens Club, backed — I believe by almost the whole, if not the whole, of the members — I have heard no discontented voices — have decided upon their course of action and have determined to take their places with the other clubs whose hope it is that future generations of sportsmen will say they did the right thing at the right time".

A Red Letter Day

The first matches in the new league were played on Saturday, 7th September, 1895 — under Rugby Union rules, and Saints began their season with a home game against Rochdale Hornets. Kick-off time was supposed to be half past three, but when the time arrived there were no teams to be seen. Doubtless some of the three thousand spectators checked their pocket watches — after all Beechams clock had been stopped all week for cleaning for the first time in six years. Half an hour later, word got around that the Hornets had missed their connection at Manchester and would be well over an hour late. One man — Charles Liptrot, certainly was not complaining. The Licensee of the Beehive Pub in Bridge Street — he had applied for an occasional license to sell 'intoxicants' on the Knowsley Road ground that afternoon and did a roaring trade in the late summer sunshine!

Eventually the waggonette carrying the two teams from the Duke of Cambridge appeared and the game commenced, at ten minutes to five, in front of a 'high spirited' crowd. The Saints were determined to make this a red-letter day for those patient supporters and took the game to the Hornets from the start. They got an early reward for their sustained pressure after a scrum on the visitors twenty-five. Bob Doherty — Saints' pint-sized winger, intercepted a pass meant for his opposite number — Uttley, swerved past Midgley and rushed for the line. He was half-tackled by full-back Wood, but broke away and rolled head over heels over the line for Saints' first try in Northern Union Football.

Although Cross failed with the conversion 'Ned' Ashcroft charged down Midgley's kick at the restart. 'Kitty' Briers led a tremendous rush to the visitors line, and Peter Dale popped out of the ruck to ground the ball under the posts for a second St. Helens try in less than a minute! Cross converted this time to give the Blue and Whites an eight - nil lead which they defended until the interval.

In the second half play was more even, the visitors for a time having the best of matters. Midgley — arguably Hornets most impressive player, kicked a penalty goal, although the result was never in much doubt. Saints supporters returned home much later than usual, but well satisfied with their team's performance. Everyone agreed that Bob Doherty had been the best St. Helens player. How he relished scoring that try! It was normally his partner on the other flank — Tom Sudlow — who grabbed the headlines.

Sudlow had another match to prepare for — of the sprinting variety! He was due to face local flier 'Jacky' Banks over 100 yards at the Starr Inn Race Grounds, Merton Bank, for the 'Championship of St. Helens'. He should have stuck to football. Banks won by a couple of yards and gleefully collected the £50 prize money!

NORTHERN UNION
Saturday, 7th September, 1895
Inaugural Fixture at Knowsley Road
ST. HELENS (8)8   ROCHDALE HORNETS (0)3

ST. HELENS: T. Foulkes, W. Whiteley, J. Appleton, J. Allan, R. Doherty 1T, W. Cross (Capt.) 1C, J. McLees, P. Dale 1T, S. Rimmer, J. Gladwin, W. Caveney, T. Reynolds, W. Briers, E. Ashcroft, J. McKay.

ROCHDALE HORNETS: J. Wood, J. Hill, S. Backley, C. Midgley 1P.G., F. Uttley, A. Mason, T. Sucksmith, P. Leach, A. Leach, J. Leach, A. Dearden, C. Trevor, F. Kershaw, A. Hill, T. Dex.

Referee: Mr. Court (Oldham)
Attendance: 3,000

The Rugby Union scoring system was used in the first couple of seasons of the Northern Union:

T	— Try (3 points)
C	— Conversion (2 points)
P.G.	— Penalty Goal (3 points)
D.G.	— Drop Goal (4 points)

At the Northern Union AGM of 1897 it was decided that every goal, however kicked, would count only two points.

An Unwanted 'First'

The Saints first Northern Union campaign was not without its problems and despite a bright start, results deteriorated. After beating Widnes 6 - 0 on Christmas Day, the team won only two of their next ten matches. The slide was halted with a 5 - 5 draw at Warrington, where new signing Billy Jacques from Hull scored a try and added the conversion.

The Committee had obtained his signature some weeks previously, on hearing that he was on a list of players 'whitewashed' by the Rugby Union. Secretary Fred Dennet knew that the 'whitewash' would make no difference if he belonged to another Northern Union Club, but his pleas to the Committee fell on deaf ears.

So St. Helens had the dubious distinction of being the first team to have points deducted in the League Competition for breaking the transfer rules. They played Jacques against Oldham on 14th December — even though he was still a registered player with the Hull club.

The Blue and Whites eventually finished fourteenth out of twenty two clubs, a moderate placing after such a promising start. Joining the Northern Union rebels had also been a costly business. In June the Committee announced a near £150 loss for the financial year. There was a new entry on the balance sheet — broken time at £106.2s.6d.

If You Can't Beat 'em

Meanwhile, the Recs had been forced to secure dates with the few first class clubs remaining under the Rugby Union — such as Swinton, Rochdale St. Clements, Leeds Parish Church and Salford. Yet there was no guarantee that these clubs would not themselves 'turn' in the near future. At the end of the season, on Saturday, 25th April, 1896 — the Recs left 'the difficult path of the pure and genuine amateur' to fraternize with the broken timers. They beat Crompton under Northern Union rules at Boundary Road in front of 1,500 spectators.

In 1896/7 the Recs played friendly matches under the new regime and hoped, eventually, to be admitted into the newly formed Lancashire Senior Competition. It was a dream that was not to materialize for over twenty years.

Striking out for a New Challenge 1896/7

The initial excitement of Saints' involvement with the Northern Union game had settled down somewhat. It was therefore, expected that interest would not be as lob-sided as the year before, especially when the Recs announced an attractive list of fixtures to whet the appetites of their followers. At the end of the season there was to be an extra incentive — a Challenge Cup Competition for Northern Union Clubs.

In rain-soaked September, this seemed rather distant from the minds of Billy Cross and his team as they made a winning start to their league campaign. Rochdale were defeated at Knowsley Road — thanks to tries by Gladwin and 'Kitty' Briers. The gloomy weather temporarily subsided, but clouds of despondency still hung over the club, owing to the mounting financial problems and rather mixed fortunes on the playing side. Matters came to a head in early October — with the following headlines in the St. Helens Newspaper:—

"Strike of the Saints forwards. The team refuses to go to Oldham".

The Saints — the report maintained, were going to be wrecked on the rock of broken time, and the Recs would look upon the wreck with reckless indifference. Yet we need not have worried. The Saints did go to Oldham with a full team and, although defeated, the difficulties had at least been resolved. The Committee blamed malicious rumours for the dissatisfaction among the forwards regarding the broken time allowance. The players had met the Executive on the Friday to state their grievances. After a patient hearing, all but three decided to play. By Saturday — only Gladwin and Ashcroft were absent from the selected eight. The Saints were, for the moment at least, a happy family once again, smiling in the face of adversity. You could not help but laugh when Billy Cross created an entertaining distraction on one fog-bound Saturday at the station, when he taxed the patience of a somewhat stern railway official by asking him many and varied questions about the train to Rochdale. "Bloody footballers......" muttered the butt of the Captain's wit "go to hell!!"

Such moments of light relief were most welcome as winter's grip tightened and the form of the Saints — and their backs in particular, gave cause for concern. Spectators howled for new blood, and the Committee promised wholesale changes to stop the rot. Predictably, this involved the solitary 'resting' of Bob Doherty from the wing. He had the reputation of being the surest tackler in the team.

This dramatic course of action had an immediate effect — things got worse! Saints opened their 1897 account on New Year's Day with a home defeat by a rampant Oldham 17 - 5. The misery continued as they crashed 20 - 0 at Runcorn twenty four hours later. The Committee, not exactly renowned for its judgement of players — promptly reinstated the hapless Doherty by public demand. Indeed, there followed a temporary upsurge in playing fortunes by early February.

The St. Helens Newspaper was in no doubt as to why there was such an improvement, in a somewhat prophetic paragraph after the defeat of lowly Salford:—

"There are some people who believe that a mud bath is an even greater specific for human ailments than the World-famous Beechams Pills — and if there be any solid ground for this belief, the St. Helens Football team may look forward to a run of success during the remaining of the season".

Such optimism proved, once again, unfounded — as the team suffered five consecutive defeats, beginning with the indignity of a reverse at the hands of Wigan. Saints supporters cursed as their train to Wigan was delayed by half an hour, but fears of missing part of the match were soon dispelled when it was found that David Traynor — the Saints' centre, was aboard. His team mates waited for him to arrive, and the kick-off was delayed by nine minutes. The return journey was untroubled — it was just the depressing result that seemed to make it even longer than before!

The blame for this recent spell of poor form lay squarely on the broad shoulders of the pack whose inept displays had given the once-maligned three-quarters little opportunity to show their renewed vigour. To its credit, the Committee had tried to strengthen this department by recruiting Joe Thompson from Kendal during the Christmas period, but this did little to impove matters overall. There was to be a welcome change of fortune on the horizon however.

Up For t'Cup

Before the disappointing league programme drew to a close came the announcement of a home draw in the first round of the Challenge Cup against a junior team — Lees "from the wilds somewhere .... with certainly not an international reputation" exclaimed the local press. Naturally, the players looked to the Cup Competition to repair their dented pride — though they would be without Billy Cross, who was out for the rest of the season with an injury. Tommy Foulkes took over the captaincy. No doubt the Committee would also welcome the extra revenue.

Against Lees — as expected, the Saints had a field day. Fourteen tries were scored. If everyone had not tried to get in on the act, the score would have been doubled! Much to the disdain of the Committee, the attendance was a meagre one. There was a more attractive fixture at Boundary Road that day where powerful Brighouse Rangers defeated the Recs in the same competition.

The second round a week later saw the visit of Castleford to Knowsley Road, when three hundred Yorkshiremen made the trek over the Pennines to make up another disappointing attendance. The howling wind deterred many spectators, especially when they discovered that normal admission prices had been doubled!

Foulkes lost the toss and St. Helens faced the gale and blinding sun. This was the chance for the heavier Yorkshire forwards to stamp their authority on the game, but it was not to be, and by the half-time whistle they led by only one try to nil. The Saints had tackled like demons with Skipper Foulkes an inspiration, and a demoralized Castleford knew they had not pressed home the advantage. Once Saints had gained initial momentum with a try by the live wire half-back O'Hara, there was no stopping them. He scored another shortly afterwards, and 'Kitty' Briers crowned the forward dominance with two further touchdowns in the 17 - 3 victory.

At last the players were showing signs of believing in themselves.

The Rebel Saints (1895 – 1901)

Anticipation was high when it was found that Wigan were the next opponents at Knowsley Road. The Wiganites were roared on by two thousand supporters on the day, but even they could not halt the march of the Saints — whose forwards were once again impressive.

Another favourable home draw in the quarter finals paired the Saints with Tyldesley. The St. Helens faithful were confident that they would have a repeat of the three previous performances, and they were not disappointed. The Saints cup bandwagon rolled unceremoniously over the 'Bongers' who were decisively beaten.

St. Helens was now in the grip of cup fever. People rushed to book their tickets for the semi-final in seven days time. Saints had drawn the Lions of Swinton — the critics choice for honours. Wheaters Field was the venue, the home of Broughton Rangers. The match had to be postponed from the Saturday to the following Monday because of bad weather. St. Helens supporters — having already arrived at Manchester on the 'specials' — were not particularly amused!

Despite the forty-eight hour delay there were enthusiastic cheers as Foulkes led his side out with over 12,000 lining the enclosure. The team looked in the pink of condition but were going to need all their stamina for the battle ahead. Right from the start both teams endeavoured to play a fast running game. In the first fifteen minutes it looked as though the crisp Swinton passing moves would prove decisive, yet there always seemed to be a St. Helens man where the ball was and the defence stood firm. Doherty in particular was terrier-like in the tackle. Gradually they were getting the upper hand and the Swinton attacks began to lack conviction.

Half-time arrived and sponges, towels and gargles were freely used during the two minutes interval, this being a concession to the players that had not been given in the earlier stages of the competition! Suitably refreshed, the Saints got down to the serious business of Lion taming. From a scrum on the Dark Blues twenty-five, Little passed to Jacques — who responded with a magnificent drop goal. The players hugged each other with delight. They were on their way.

The end to end nature of the play continued up until the last quarter of the match when luck deserted Swinton. Their Captain Valentine — collided with a brick wall called Whiteley and seven minutes later he was carried off in obvious discomfort. Goodman was taken out of the pack to replace him and this proved to be their undoing. From a line out close to the Swinton line, Little snatched the ball and dummied his way over. Many Swintonians in the crowd had long since begun their journey home when Referee Holmes of Manningham 'reduced to a condition of limp perspiration' blew the final whistle. The unbelievable had happened. Wheaters Field had not seen the like before as players, officials and spectators celebrated in grand style.

'Spectator' in the St. Helens Newspaper remarked on the incredible pace of the match. Foulkes was praised for a faultless performance, Traynor being singled out as the best three-quarter on the field. Apart from the poor Swinton Captain it was found that Sutton had broken his collar bone, thus necessitating the first team change of the competition for the final.

Battle of the Roses

In the grandstand sat some of the players and officials of Saints opponents in the final, Batley. The 'Gallant Youths' from Yorkshire were under no illusions as to the size of their task. Luckily for them the match was to be played at Headingley, Leeds — described by a local writer as "The handsomest rugby enclosure in England" — though hardly a neutral venue in the true sense!

Confidence had been high in the St. Helens camp all week, despite Sutton's accident on the Monday. Indeed such were the exertions of the players in the semi-final that they had barely recuperated. The Batleyites had the advantage of a couple of days extra rest, while some of the Lancastrians were carrying minor injuries. 'Pug' Whiteley's arm had been in a sling for most of the week, but that was not going to worry him and he declared himself fit on the morning of the match.

The team and their officials, plus fifty of their staunchest supporters left for Leeds by the ten past nine train. Arriving in the city at noon, they had lunch and were later conveyed to the Headingley ground. Fine weather now prevailed, despite a threatening morning and the players inspected a pitch in perfect condition. Around them was a stadium that could accommodate well over twenty thousand spectators with its large stands and banks providing an excellent view.

In the tense dressing room the various Saints went through their normal pre-match preparations. They were a superstitious lot and Cup Final or not, the routine was to be the same. Five minutes to kick-off, and outside a crowd of thirteen and a half thousand licked their lips in anticipation. The nerves began to jangle even more. After a final few words of encouragement from Billy Cross, the Saints bounded on to the field to somewhat muted cheers. They were wearing what the Athletic News called 'faded and washed out blue and white jerseys'. These were the same jerseys they had worn with such distinction all through the cup run. They had brought them luck, and a change was out of the question. It is doubtful whether the Committee would have bought new kit anyhow! Another cheer — this time of much larger volume, heralded the appearance of the pride of Batley, clad in spotless brand new white shirts. Both teams then submitted themselves to the photographer and five minutes after official kick-off time, the game commenced.

Foulkes won the choice of ends and decided to take advantage of the strong wind. Even at this early stage the 'Gallant Youths' surprised the jittery Saints by the aggression of their forwards. This pressure bore fruit when from a scrum, fly-half Oakland just managed to drop a goal with an oblique kick. The cheers were deafening and one startled youngster took a tumble from his improvised vantage point in a neighbouring tree. Despite being laid out tackling Fitzgerald, Foulkes recovered quickly and found himself busy keeping his line intact.

After a spell of pressure, the ball was sent out by Oakland and H. Goodall to Wattie Davies who screwed a kick from the touchline to the opposite posts. John Goodall, apparently off-side, had only to catch the ball and canter over the line. The Skipper quietly cursed his team's bad fortune — but contined to encourage his players.

It was estimated that just under one thousand 'Sintelliners' set out for the match but, unfortunately, the two excursion trains took nearly three hours to do the journey. When the trippers reached the field they were doubly depressed by their favourites seven points deficit. As Saints at last seemed to recover from their nervousness, good chances were wasted, especially by O'Hara who missed a kickable penalty and failed with a drop goal attempt.

The outlook was bleak when the Saints had to face the wind and a seven points lead. Early in the second half however, they maintained their reputation for playing better against the wind. That is until Lady Luck struck another cruel blow, when Fitzgerald clashed with Little who had no option but to hobble off the pitch in some distress. 'Kitty' Briers was moved out of the pack to replace him and, like Swinton in the semi-final, the Saints ardour was dampened even more.

Although the beleaguered Lancastrians needed a near miracle they were not finished yet. The bustling Batley 'eight' took the game once again to the Saints twenty-five. Goodall tried to drop a goal, but sliced his effort straight to Doherty, who fielded the ball and shrugged off Fitzgerald's and Davies's attempted tackles. A dummy to the supporting Jacques, a quick turn and a lovely timed pass fizzed out to Traynor. The auburn haired Widnesian ran like a frightened stag along the touchline, hotly pursued by Garner and Davies. Goodall and Shaw tried to cut him off, but he brushed them aside splendidly, eventually running a few yards nearer the posts, grounding the ball just as he was tackled. It was a try more than worthy of the occasion and the spontaneous applause showed how highly his feat was appreciated. Much to the disgust of his Captain, Jacques failed to convert, but the try had a wonderful effect on Little — who hopped back on to the field. He was more of a liability however, and once or twice he seemed to prevent Doherty from taking passes which might have made openings. This, together with a pack still weakened by Briers' withdrawal, meant that the Batley team were scarcely ever outside the Saints twenty-five until the finish. Munns clinched the proceedings when he scored from a scramble at the corner flag. The game was over some time before the final whistle declared Batley — the first winners of the Northern Union Cup.

'Philistine' in the Athletic News, concluded that the Batley forward power had been the major factor on the day:—

"The Batley forwards were too strong and too bull-necked for the men from St. Helens, and the style in which the ultimate victors began their work told a tale in the first twenty minutes. Seven points to the good in that period against the wind was worth nearly seventy in the matter of enthusiasm, and Batley played like winners from the start".

A most disconsolate Foulkes sportingly congratulated his opposite number and the superb trophy was presented to J. B. Goodall by Mrs. Waller, wife of the President of the Northern Union. The Saints ruefully collected their runners-up medals and reflected on what might have been. David Traynor received special praise for his marvellous score, fully justified too, as it was the one and only time the Batley line had been crossed during the competition.

Back in the dressing room a certain St. Helens player — who had not exactly displayed his true form, changed in record time and made a suspiciously quick exit. "The bugger had been got at" — snarled Tommy Foulkes some years later.

The two teams were taken to the Exchange Restaurant for tea, and the jubilant Batley contingent left for home by the seven thirty train. The first notification of their arrival in the town was the discharge of one hundred and sixty fog signals along the line. The Batley Old Band promptly escorted them to a heroes welcome at the Town Hall.

The sad Saints went home to a more restrained welcome. Although their name would not be inscribed on the cup they had at least played their part in creating a bit of history. No doubt they were to relive the match countless times in their dreams. Little did they know it was destined to be a recurring nightmare.

CHALLENGE CUP FINAL
Saturday, 24th April, 1897
At Headingley, Leeds
ST. HELENS (0)3   BATLEY (7)10

ST. HELENS: T. Foulkes (Capt.), R. Doherty, D. Traynor 1T, J. Barnes, R. O'Hara, F. Little, T. Winstanley, W. Briers, W. Winstanley, T. Reynolds, J. Thompson, P. Dale, S. Rimmer, W. Whiteley.

BATLEY: A. Garner, W. Davies, D. Fitzgerald, J. Goodall (Capt.) 1T, J. Shaw, J Oakland 1DG, H. Goodall, M. Shackleton, J. Gath, G. Maine, F. Fisher, C. Stubley, J. Littlewood, J. T. Munns 1T.

Referee: Mr. Smith (Widnes)
Attendance: 13,492
Receipts: £624.17s.7d.

A COMPARISON OF AGE/HEIGHT/WEIGHT OF THE ST. HELENS AND BATLEY TEAMS

ST. HELENS:

NAME	AGE	HEIGHT	WEIGHT	POSITION
T. Foulkes	25	5' 7"	11.10	Full-back
R. Doherty	28	5' 4"	10. 6	Three-quarters
J. Barnes	21	5' 9"	10.10	,, ,,
D. Traynor	22	5' 8"	12. 4	,, ,,
W. Jacques	22	5' 6"	10.10	,, ,,
R. O'Hara	21	5' 5"	11. 0	Half-back
F. Little	26	5' 4"	10.11	,, ,,
W. Briers	22	5' 6½"	11.11	Forward
P. Dale	25	5' 7"	12. 7	,,
T. Reynolds	27	5' 10"	12. 4	,,
S. Rimmer	27	5' 7½"	12. 0	,,
J. Thompson	24	5' 8½"	12. 0	,,
W. Whiteley	25	5' 9"	12. 2	,,
T. Winstanley	26	5' 11"	14. 1	,,
W. Winstanley	26	5' 7"	12. 8	,,

BATLEY:

NAME	AGE	HEIGHT	WEIGHT	POSITION
A. Garner	26	5' 7"	10. 7	Full-back
W. Davies	23	5' 5"	11. 6	Three-quarters
D. Fitzgerald	24	5' 11"	12. 0	,, ,,
J. B. Goodall	22	5' 7"	11. 4	,, ,,
I. Shaw	29	5' 6"	10. 4	,, ,,
J. Oakland	21	5' 8"	11. 0	Half-back
H. Goodall	23	5' 7½"	11. 7	,, ,,
M. Shackleton	27	6' 0"	14. 0	Forward
J. Gath	21	5' 9"	11. 7	,,
G. Maine	21	5' 7"	10.11	,,
R. Spurr	23	5' 11"	12. 7	,,
F. Fisher	24	5' 8"	13. 8	,,
C. Stubley	27	5' 7"	12. 7	,,
J. Littlewood	23	5' 9"	12. 0	,,
J. T. Munns	22	5' 9"	13. 4	,,

The Rebel Saints (1895 – 1901)

Batley had a slight height and weight average. William Briers could be described as the 'average' St. Helens player in terms of physique of 5' 7" and 11st 11 lbs.

It is interesting to compare the 1897 player statistics with those of a more contemporary era, in this case the 1972 Challenge Cup winning team. Nowhere is the difference in height and weight more marked than in the pack.

The 1897 Saints forward is four inches and three stones lighter on average than his twentieth century counterpart.

	Average Height		Average Weight	
	1897	1972	1897	1972
Three-quarter backs	5' 7"	5' 9½"	11. 2	12. 5
Half-backs	5' 4"	5' 7"	10.12	11.00
Forwards	5' 8"	6' 0"	12. 6	15.12
TEAM	5' 7"	5' 9½"	11.11	13. 4

Doubtless the Batley Cup finalists would have faced a forward like John Mantle – 6' 2" and 15st 4 lbs. with great respect and more than a little trepidation.

The Batley Bogey

Everyone did their level best to put that Cup Final defeat behind them, and Saints began the 1897-98 season in good shape. Alas, it was too good to last. The side struck a patch of bad form that included six consecutive defeats from mid-October to December, dashing any hopes of league success.

The disappointed Committee, ever mindful of the lack of cash, were pinning their hopes on another lengthy cup run to swell the coffers. There were to be a few furrowed brows as, by a remarkable coincidence, the draw for the first round of the Northern Union Cup brought together the previous years finalists. Once again good fortune had favoured Batley and the game was to be played on their own Mount Pleasant ground.

A comparison of the records of the two sides, prior to the cup tie, is shown below:—

					For		Ag	
	P	W	D	L	G	T	P	G	T	P
ST. HELENS	22	9	0	13	16	31	125	25	38	166
BATLEY	26	14	3	9	26	51	205	17	22	100

As their impressive league form shows, Batley were obvious favourites, especially with home advantage.

A full strength St. Helens team, eager for revenge, journeyed to Huddersfield in a saloon carriage and had dinner at the Crown Hotel, afterwards proceeding to the Batley ground. Every seat in the grandstand was taken as the kick-off drew near, with one exception. One of the stewards distinguished himself by making the then President and main supporter of the Batley club pay his entrance money because he left his season ticket at home. The President fumed, but he paid all right!

His team had more luck and won the toss, electing to play with the wind at their backs. Quite early on O'Hara was penalized for feeding near his own line and the Tykes opened their account with a Davies penalty goal.

Despite this early setback the Saints impressed with their defence, even if it was a little over-zealous at times. As half-time approached and frustration was at its height, the Gallant Youths got the vital break. It came from a most unexpected source. Tommy Foulkes of all people let a ball slip through his hands and Shackleton followed up to score. Davies converted and soon after Traynor made mistake number two by kicking weakly into J. Goodall's hands. He responded gleefully with a magnificent drop goal.

After the break, playing with all the aid of the breeze, St. Helens hoped to put a different complexion on the game. Batley were soon pressed back on the defensive. Traynor should have scored easily at one point, but dropped the ball. It was up to O'Hara to lift Lancastrian hopes as he dribbled away and fed Doherty. 'Bob Doc' raced over for a splendid try converted by Traynor.

The exchanges certainly became fierce, especially in the final quarter as Batley held on to their lead. The game erupted at one point when Jim Barnes tried to knock the unfortunate Davies back to Wales and received his marching orders. A furious finale saw Traynor reduce the arrears with a penalty goal from a mark. Twelve points to seven, and Batley hearts were fluttering as Rutter was held inches from the line seconds before the final whistle. But it was not to be Saints' day. The Batley Bogey had struck again.

Fourteen disgruntled Saints trudged off the field cursing the two errors that had cost them the game. Yet they had played reasonably well under the circumstances. Spectators and even Policemen on duty had assisted the Tykes by kicking the ball down the steep slope adjoining the ground whenever it came out of play and St. Helens were pressing.

The Batley Boys had overcome their most formidable hurdle, and they went on to retain the trophy by beating local rivals Bradford 7 - 0 at Headingley, fast becoming their second home. The crowd and receipts were to double from the first match.

St. Helens wingman Bob Doherty shared a unique distinction with Traynor, his fellow three-quarter from the year before. His marvellous effort at Mount Pleasant was also the only try Batley were to concede in the competition. Another remarkable coincidence and testimony to the fact that althought twice beaten, the Saints had made them fight all the way.

CHALLENGE CUP – FIRST ROUND
Saturday, 26th February, 1898
At Mount Pleasant, Batley
BATLEY (12)12   ST. HELENS (0)7

ST. HELENS: T. Foulkes (Capt.), Rutter, R. Doherty 1T, D. Traynor 2G, J. Barnes, W. Cross, R. O'Hara, T. Winstanley, W. Whiteley, W. Briers, J. Thompson, J. Gladwin, J. Simpson, P. Dale, J. Taylor.

BATLEY: Garner, Fozzard, J. B. Goodall (Capt.) 1T, 1G, Davies 2G, Eddison, H. Goodall, Oakland, Shackleton 1T, Gath, Stubley, Mann, Rodgers, Phillips, Munns, Spurr.

Referee: Mr. Priestley (Salford)
Attendance: 5,000

Defeat of the Rough'yeds

In today's game there is a much greater emphasis on speed for both backs and forwards. The modern forward in particular cannot afford to carry as much surplus weight as his predecessors. Players like Bob Eccles have the physical attributes to cope with the rigours of a prop and second row forward, yet can also reveal a devastating turn of speed. As the pace has tended to even out between forwards and backs it is much easier for players to alternate positions.

In the early days of the Northern Union the forwards mauled and scrimmaged to get the ball to the three-quarters who had the pace. Fast forwards were a rarity, but Saints had in their pack William Briers, a man with a reputation for strength and speed. 'Kitty' as he was known could also do 100 yards in eleven seconds. Tommy Foulkes recalled the many bright sovereigns they took from visiting teams and spectators when they wanted to back their opinion that Kitty could not do it. He was also considered to be one of the greatest dribblers of a ball that the game has ever seen. Indeed he once scored a try against Runcorn by dribbling virtually the whole length of the field.

When Oldham visited Knowsley Road on 1st October, 1898 they did so as reigning champions of Lancashire. The previous season they had lost only two out of twenty-six games. It was easy to see why they had such an invincible reputation. Their supporters gave Saints no earthly chance. They would be beaten out of sight with consummate ease.

How wrong they were! The scintillating Saints tore the Cotton Spinners to shreds by fifteen points to nine. It was a magnificent team performance and a personal triumph for 'Kitty' Briers. Showing his versatility by playing as a half-back he roared in for three tries. He had Joe Thompson to thank for his first, as the Staveley man charged a kick down for 'Kitty' to dash over. He completed his hat-trick by using his forward's instincts, grounding the ball twice after superb rushes from his pack. What a magnificent performance from 'Kitty' Briers, in many ways a man ahead of his time.

To their credit, a stunned Oldham side accepted defeat like true gentlemen. They later presented Briers with a special cap to mark his achievement, and got their revenge later in the season to the tune of sixteen points to nil.

LANCASHIRE SENIOR COMPETITION
Saturday, 1st October, 1898
At Knowsley Road
ST. HELENS (15)15   OLDHAM (0)9

ST. HELENS: T. Foulkes (Capt.), R. Doherty, J. Barnes, D. Traynor 3G, Siddall, W. Briers 3T, Boyle, P. Dale, W. Whiteley, J. Simpson, T. Reynolds, Stubbings, W. Winstanley, J. Thompson, J. Chapman.

OLDHAM: Wood, Thomas 1T, T. Davies, S. Lees, Williams 2T, Lawton, Rees, Bonser, Frater, Porter, F. Davies, J. Lees, Edwards, Murrell, Broome.

Wagons—Ho for a Ham Bonus

On Saturday 2nd September, 1899 in the opening match of the season, Warrington held St. Helens to a three-all draw at Knowsley Road. Tommy Foulkes, his close pal 'Kitty' Briers and Bill Whiteley, boarded the horse-drawn waggonette that would take both teams back to the club headquarters at the Duke of Cambridge Hotel.

As the wagon trundled through the cobbled streets, they chatted about times gone by. Tommy Foulkes remembered when the team had been given an enormous ham to raffle. The ticket money was shared out among the players, a welcome bonus as they sometimes did not get paid at all for playing.

One bonus they had certainly earned was for beating Swinton in the cup semi-final at Broughton in 1897. 'Kitty' Briers thought it was the most exciting game he had ever played in. Bill Whiteley smiled ruefully as he remembered his fateful clash with the Lions' Captain that day. He suppressed a shudder as his thoughts turned to the winter months ahead. Bill hated the return journey in the waggonette on a cold, wet day. He frequently ran back to headquarters instead, in his soggy playing togs. Defeat on such a day only added to his misery. A mild winter with good home results would suit the quiet north countryman down to the ground.

The opening draw with the Wirepullers proved to be one of the few hiccups during the first half of the season. By Christmas, St. Helens had lost only four matches and, at one stage, completed a sequence of seven straight wins. 1st January, 1900 was a double cause for celebration. The sizzling Saints welcomed in the new century with a crushing twenty-six – nil victory over Leigh. They never really looked back and their good form in the Lancashire Senior Competition was rewarded with fourth place in the table.

LANCASHIRE SENIOR COMPETITION
Final Table 1899/1900 (Top four clubs)

	P	W	D	L	F	A	Pts
Runcorn	26	22	2	2	232	33	46
Oldham	26	21	1	4	340	75	43
Swinton	26	19	1	6	210	108	39
St. Helens	26	16	3	7	207	119	35

St. Helens Record against the Top Three Clubs

v	Runcorn	(A)	Lost	0 - 9
		(H)	Won	3 - 2
v	Oldham	(A)	Lost	6 - 35
		(H)	Won	17 - 14
v	Swinton	(A)	Drew	0 - 0
		(H)	Won	17 - 3

Saints could hold their own with all the top clubs at home. The Oldham match at Knowsley Road saw no less than five tries from the homesters. A rare treat indeed!

A New Challenge

The one major disappointment of the campaign was another failure in the Challenge Cup, when Warrington beat them in the first round by six points to nil at Knowsley Road. However, there was a chance for some consolation, for a new competition – 'The South West Lancs. and Border Towns Cup' – had been rushed through the last few weeks of the season. Originally eight teams put their names down, but Swinton and Warrington later withdrew. This left St. Helens, Leigh, Wigan, Tyldesley, Widnes and Runcorn.

The Saints did themselves no harm at all by defeating Leigh and Widnes to reach the final. Their opponents were to be Runcorn, who had beaten Wigan in their only game of the competition so far.

Could Saints do it? Runcorn had swept all before them in the league and were worthy champions. It would take a magnificent team performance to overcome them, but Tommy Foulkes and the lads were quietly confident.

They knew that a Cup Final was a different matter altogether.

The final took place on the evening of Monday 29th April at Widnes, before a crowd of about three thousand spectators. In a surprisingly scoreless first half St. Helens defended resolutely, despite having the strong wind and blinding sun against them. Foulkes was his usual capable self at full-back.

The second-half was marked by the fine defensive play of the Runcornians. Later on they lost Farmer and Tomlinson with injuries, but their green line held firm until the final whistle.

It was decided to play seven and a half minutes extra time each way. Saints attacked with renewed vigour and made the vital breakthrough with an Appleton try. After the change of ends, St. Helens clinched the proceedings when Jim Barnes scored a cracking try with a brilliant run half the length of the field.

The jubilation in the Saints' camp was captured in the following day's edition of the St. Helens Newspaper:—

> "The cup was presented to T. Foulkes by Mr. J. H. Smith of Widnes, in a neat little speech and, after the team had passed the cup round and lightened its burden of champagne, Foulkes appropriately responded".

It is a shame that Saints' first trophy win under Northern Union rules has gone largely unrecognized. People at the time tended to dismiss the competition as meaningless. They argued that Runcorn did not extend themselves fully in the final. Quite rightly the Saints Committee would have none of it! They were proud of their team's achievement and looked forward to further success in the future.

SOUTH WEST LANCS. AND BORDER TOWNS CUP FINAL
Monday, 29th April, 1900
At Widnes
ST. HELENS (0)0   RUNCORN (0)0
ST. HELENS WON 6 - 0 AFTER EXTRA TIME

ST. HELENS: T. Foulkes (Capt.), R. Doherty, J. Barnes 1T, D. Traynor, G. Liversage, Boyle, J.Appleton 1T, W. Briers, P. Dale, W. Whiteley, J. Thompson, F. Melvin, W. Prescott, W. Green, Rennie.

RUNCORN: Houghton, Jones, J. Butterworth, Warder, C. Butterworth, Richardson, Jolley, Farmer, Darlington, Hughes, Walker, Taylor, Langley, Gayter, Tomlinson.

Attendance: 3,000

In the Pink

The 1899-1900 season was the most successful the town club had ever known, both from a financial and a playing point of view. Certainly the club was never better managed, and the players were a marvellously enthusiastic bunch. Performance had been all the more creditable considering they received the smallest wages in the competition. "It was as though they were drawing Oldham's salaries every week" observed the Athletic News wryly.

The improvement in the playing side had stabilized matters financially. At the Annual Meeting the Treasurer was able to announce that they had made a profit of £126 on the past year's work, and could show a balance of £62 to the credit of the club.

There had been improvements to the ground and plans were revealed for a new popular side stand. A ten thousand crowd could now be accommodated at Knowsley Road.

The Saints and Bob Doc

It was early August, 1900 and the Saints were enduring the twice weekly routine of practice matches and sprints. They were all determined to carry on where they had left off the previous season. Bob Doherty, the tough little three-quarter was no exception. Since joining St. Helens from Kendal Hornets almost ten years before, the local rugbyites had taken 'Bob Doc' to their hearts. His tackling for a small man was exceptional and he could bring down opponents forty or fifty pounds heavier than himself. Bob Doc and David Traynor always tried to be one step ahead of the opposition, and were early exponents of the 'loop' move. Traynor would give his team mate a short pass then run round into space along the touchline side to receive the return. The deadly duo picked up a bagful of tries in this fashion!

The Losing Streak

Even though early results were encouraging, experience had taught the St. Helens spectators to take nothing for granted. Such guarded optimism was warranted when their team visited Oldham on 13th October. There was to be no glory for Billy Briers and the boys this time as the Roughyeds coasted to a 22 - 2 victory.

The defeat proved to be a significant watershed for the Saints. Morale was shattered to such an extent that unfancied Millom triumphed at Knowsley Road a week later. A draw at Wigan did little to restore confidence. Soon after, Salford and Warrington came away from the home of the 'Saintly Sinners' with the points. It was the start of a series of reversals unparalleled in the club's early history.

Blame was heaped upon the forwards who, not long before, used to be the pride of the club. The St. Helens Newspaper decided that there were some 'luggards' in the pack who would benefit by at least a temporary rest.

They should be quickly replaced by 'more energetic' men.

The pressure began to tell on one Saints forward who held a running disagreement with his Warrington counterpart during the Wirepullers' victory at Knowsley Road. The quarrel was later renewed in the waggonette after the match, where the St. Helens contender laid his opponent out. Under normal circumstances such unsaintly behaviour was quite rare of course!

The Committee's response to the crisis showed a predictable lack of judgement. By the end of November they were looking to improve the back division, despite the fact that the forwards had been continuously outplayed since early October.

The fortnightly meeting of the League Management Committee in Manchester on Tuesday, 27th November, brought further bad tidings. Liversage — the Saints' three-quarter had changed his employment. The club had neglected to inform the Northern Union Secretary as per competition rule 28. They were fined heavily for this oversight and had two points deducted from their league total.

St. Helens were certainly going down with a vengeance. Defeats by Oldham, Broughton, Leigh, Widnes and at Warrington in the South West Lancs. and Border Towns Cup, followed in quick succession. There was to be some respite for the ailing 'Sintelliners' however. Huddersfield were defeated in a friendly on New Year's Day by a side showing several changes. These included Charlie Creevey from Pocket Nook Shamrocks, on the wing, and Lomax from Warrington at half-back.

The long list of defeats actually roused the St. Helens officials into taking positive action. The players were put under regular training rules, and the result was quickly seen. At Barrow they were leading until the last ten minutes, while at Leigh, they were somewhat unlucky to be beaten by five points.

Bob Doc the Lion Tamer

On the afternoon of Saturday, 19th January, 1901 — the rain pelted down outside the Duke of Cambridge. Bob Doherty, as depressed as the weather with his own poor form, prepared for the match against Swinton. He reflected on the irony of the situation as he boarded the waggonette. Saints had lost ten successive matches. The Lions had not yet been beaten in the competition, and wanted to remain so.

The teams arrived at a wet and windy Knowsley Road and inspected the pitch, which in parts resembled a quagmire. Bob Doc knew they were in with a good chance of breaking the losing spell. The heavy going would certainly slow down the visiting three-quarters.

Swinton won the toss and took the opportunity of playing with the wind at their backs. Saints were put under constant pressure and were grateful to Tommy Foulkes who managed to keep the home line intact. Conditions certainly did not suit the fast and clever Swinton team, who were not allowed to play their normal open game. Saints forwards, ably led by 'Kitty' Briers, rushed, dribbled and kept the ball close.

As the second half began, all Swinton had to show for their pressure was a solitary try. Anything but dismayed by the three point margin, 'Kitty' led his forwards into the fray with renewed vigour. Foulkes was in brilliant form, catching Chorley or Valentine's relieving kicks and driving his opponents back again.

Eventually the pressure paid off. Cross, playing in the forwards, dribbled away from a ruck. He screwed the ball across the goal line where Tom Briers, brother of Billy, touched down. Although Barnes missed the goal, Saints continued to bombard the Dark Blue line.

The game was in its last quarter when a scrum was formed fifteen yards from the Swinton line. Saints heeled the ball out cleanly. Unsworth picked up and fed Appleton. He passed it to Traynor, who gave it to Bob Doc and the little fellow swerved past the clutches of Hampson and Valentine and dived in at the corner to score the winning try.

The same principle applied in the early 1900's as it does today. A heavy ground is a real leveller of clubs and goes a long way to bring the stars and crocks together.

Bob Doc's super score had not only broken the terrible sequence of results, he also earned the undying gratitude of Oldham, who were chasing Swinton in second place in the table. Swinton were so upset that they complained to the League about the state of the pitch, but to no avail. Indeed the Rough'yeds later went on to win the title by a single point!

SWINTON FOOTBALL CLUB
Swinton, Manchester
21st January, 1901

Swinton v St. Helens — 19th January, 1901

Dear Sir — I beg to inform you that I have this day lodged a protest to the Lancashire Senior Competition against the Swinton v St. Helens match, played on Saturday last being considered a competition match, on the grounds that the field was not fit for such. Rule 23 'Lancashire·Senior Competition Rules' states "that if any doubt arises as to the fitness of any ground, the Secretary of the home club must advise the visiting club as early as possible to send a deputation to inspect the ground, and upon inspection — should the two clubs fail to agree, the Referee — who shall also be advised to attend, shall have full power to decide whether the match be played or not etc. etc."

It was not until our players and officials arrived on the field at 2.56 p.m. that the state of the field was seen, and spectators were then on the ground. Also Rule 11 states "that the Committee shall have full power to deal with any offending club or clubs, player or players — as they may think fit, and they shall also have power to deal with any matter that arises in connection with the competition that is not provided for in these rules and bye-laws". I have deposited the fee of £5.

Yours truly

C. PLATT
Secretary

LETTER OF COMPLAINT
SENT BY SWINTON TO THE LEAGUE
AFTER DEFEAT BY THE SAINTS ON 19th JANUARY, 1901.
THE PROTEST WAS UPHELD

As for poor old Saints, their abysmal run was only briefly halted. They finished second from bottom and had to play Widnes at Warrington to decide who should be holders of the wooden spoon. The losers also had to appear in a 'Test Match' with Morecambe, who were hoping to regain their lost position in the 'upper circle'.

Saints at least avoided both those unwanted distinctions, thanks to a three points to nil victory. The try was another splendid effort down the wing by Dob Doc, who had only scored two tries during the season — but what important ones they proved to be.

LANCASHIRE SENIOR COMPETITION

Final Table — 1900-01

		P	W	D	L	F	A	Pts
1	Oldham	26	22	1	3	301	67	45
2	Swinton	26	21	2	3	283	66	44
3	Runcorn	26	20	0	6	240	100	40
4	Broughton R	26	17	2	7	211	84	36
5	Salford	26	15	0	11	229	149	30
6	Warrington	26	12	3	11	149	126	27
7	Leigh	26	12	2	12	157	143	26
8	Barrow	26	10	2	14	140	169	22
9	Wigan	26	8	3	15	98	227	19
10	Rochdale H	26	8	2	16	103	257	18
11	Millom	26	8	0	18	85	194	16
12	Stockport	26	6	3	17	102	184	15
13	St. Helens +	26	6	2	18	82	228	12
14	Widnes	26	6	0	20	85	271	12

+ Two points deducted for a breach of the professional rules.

The Batley Bogey Strikes again

Saints looked to the Challenge Cup for a change of fortune. In front of six thousand spectators at Knowsley Road, St. Helens lost to their old adversary Batley in the third round by five points to seven. The match was very exciting and the result was in the balance up to the final whistle. As the players left the field, more fun was to follow.

Let the St. Helens Newspaper take up the story:—

"Words were passed between one or two of the Batley players and some of the St. Helens supporters. The outcome was that blows were struck and Goodall, one of the Batley three-quarters, appeared to be the chief object of the wrath of a section of the crowd. It is alleged that Goodall, Hollingworth and Mr. Shaw, the Batley Secretary, were all roughly handled. It was with some difficulty that the players reached the waggonette which conveyed them to the head-quarters of the St. Helens club and they were followed by a large crowd. Eventually, several officers appeared on the scene and the crowd was dispersed. The Police Officers afterwards accompanied the Batley players to the railway station".

History had repeated itself with a vengeance once more, and the frustration of the spectators was understandable, their subsequent behaviour inexcusable. Batley went on to lift the cup just as before, beating Warrington 6 - 0 at Headingley. A disconsolate Tommy Foulkes felt that his chances of captaining his team to a Challenge Cup Final victory had gone for good. He was very much in the veteran stage, and time was no longer on his side.

Tommy Foulkes never did achieve his dearest ambition. Nor did he see a Saints team win the cup. Indeed it was two years after his death in 1955 that the Batley Bogey was exorcised for good. Times had changed — Saints were in the ascendancy now and gloom hung over Mount Pleasant. The side was struggling at the foot of the table, support had dwindled and money was scarce. Despite the infamous Batley sloping pitch, St. Helens won comfortably by 15 - 2. Carlton scored two tries, Finnan the other — with Joe Ball kicking three goals.

CHALLENGE CUP — THIRD ROUND
Saturday, 23rd March, 1901
At Knowsley Road
ST. HELENS (5)5   BATLEY (5)7

ST. HELENS: T. Foulkes (Capt.), R. Doherty, Hunter 1T, D. Traynor 1G, G. Liversage, J. Appleton, J. Morris, W. Briers, J. Thompson, W. Winstanley, P. Dale, W. Cross, T. Briers, W. Whiteley, F. Melvin.

BATLEY: Garner, Davies 1T, 1G, Fitzgerald 1G, Goodall, Fozzard, Oakland (Capt.), Midgeley, Fisher, Spurr, Stubley, Rodgers, Maine, Carroll, Judge, Hollingworth.

Referee: Mr. Renton (Hunslet)
Attendance: 5,500

Chapter 3
The Yo-Yo Saints (1902 — 1906)

No Work ..... No Play

Since the first season of the Northern Union, there had been several rule changes to improve play for the spectators. From 1897 all goals counted two points, and the line-out had been abolished for a kick-in from touch. This punt-out was itself replaced by a ten yard scrum.

Clubs were warned that they would be fined if they did not start their matches on time.

As attendances increased, players realized their value as crowd pullers and agitated for higher rates of broken time payments. In 1898, professionalism was adopted. A player could now be paid as much as his club thought he was worth. The Northern Union authorities however, were determined that no-one should make his living from the game, and they introduced a working clause which insisted that players had to have legitimate employment in a full-time job. Specifically excluded were billiard markers, waiters in licensed houses and any employment in connection with a club.

Irvin Saxton in the Rugby Leaguer explained some further conditions of the clause:—

> *"A player who lost his job could not play until he was back in work, and anyone out of work due to fire, lockout or strike, had to apply to the Northern Union for permission to play. All the professionals, together with details of their employment, had to be registered by club secretaries with the Union".*

As we have seen with the Liversage affair, punishment was severe. Two league points were deducted for any club found guilty of breaking the professional rules. Gradually however, the Northern Union became more lenient towards infringements of the working clause. Even so, some decisions certainly lacked compassion. Saints' three-quarter Jones had been off work on the morning of the league match with Rochdale on the 19th December, 1903 — owing to his wife being seriously ill. St. Helens officials were quite satisfied that the cause of absence was bona-fide and he was allowed to play that afternoon. The Northern Union Sub-Committee did not agree. Jones was suspended for a month and the Rochdale game replayed.

State of the Union

In the later stages of the 1900-01 season, certain clubs campaigned for a new 'Super League' that would contain the top teams from the Lancashire and Yorkshire competitions. Despite some opposition, the new Northern

League was formed at a meeting of the interested clubs in Huddersfield in May, 1901. St. Helens did not attend and were not invited to join the new organization.

The Northern League consisted of fourteen members — Hull, Hunslet, Huddersfield, Halifax, Batley, Bradford, Brighouse Rangers, Oldham, Swinton, Salford, Broughton Rangers, Warrington, Leigh and Runcorn. The championship was a one-horse race. Broughton Rangers had clinched the title by February. They later lifted the Challenge Cup for good measure.

The Yorkshire Senior Competition Clubs boycotted fixtures against those in the new league, but in Lancashire the change was accepted as inevitable and St. Helens continued as members of the Lancashire Senior Competition, reconstructed by the invitation of several Lancashire Second Competition Clubs. A surprise addition was Hull Kingston Rovers, who were fed-up with the attitude of Yorkshire clubs towards the new league.

Saints finished third to champions Wigan, with the much travelled Yorkshiremen in fifth place. Lancashire clubs left out of the 'Super League' could play Northern League teams in two new competitions, the South West Lancashire and South East Lancashire competitions. Poor St. Helens finished bottom of the former, winning two games out of ten. The Knowsley Road faithful resigned themselves to another season away from the Northern League elite.

The club was not in the top bracket financially, that's for sure, as Tom Reynolds ('Premier' of the St. Helens Newspaper) recalled many years later:—

> "Saints were due to visit Hull K.R. in a Cup Tie in 1902. They had the skips, they had the men, they had the money too, but not at that moment. The money was still to come, after the match. Puzzle — How were the Saints to get to Hull to play the match to earn the money that was still to come? Has a railway company a soul? I don't know, but this much is clear — there was an LMS Station Master in St. Helens who had. He met the transport problem by allowing the St. Helens team to travel 'on strap' on condition they that paid for their tickets with their share of the gate when they came back".

And Then There Were Two!

The successful new Northern League signalled the end of the parochial county competitions, so much so that a second division was proposed. A Northern League meeting on 17th June, 1902 accepted applications for membership from Leeds, York, Wakefield Trinity, Manningham, Dewsbury, Holbeck, Bramley, Keighley, Normanton, Castleford, Hull K.R., Morcambe, St. Helens, Barrow, Widnes, South Shields, Millom, Rochdale Hornets, Stockport, Birkenhead and Lancaster.

Wigan were granted a first division place by virtue of being the

The Yo-Yo Saints (1902 – 1906)

Lancashire Senior Competition champions. Brighouse Rangers, bottom of the Northern League the previous year were re-admitted. The remaining three places would be voted for by all thirty-six clubs. As many ballots as necessary would be held with the club with least votes dropping out each time.

The voting was held on 1st July. Clubs who wanted to be in the first division had been canvassing for votes. Those former members of the Yorkshire Senior Competition who knew they would be in the second division anyway, voted consistently for South Shields, Widnes and St. Helens. This was not out of brotherly love, more an attempt to reduce travelling expenses! Leeds, themselves Yorkshire Senior Competition Champions, could not muster enough votes — and remained in the second division. Widnes, Hull K.R. and a jubilant St. Helens were duly elected into the top flight.

Saints were indeed grateful for good old Yorkshire thrift. The question was, were they good enough to stay there?

How the voting went:—

BALLOT:	1	2	3	4	5	6	7
Manningham	9	9	8	10	10	—	—
Stockport	5	5	—	—	—	—	—
Wakefield	8	9	7	—	—	—	—
Leeds	13	11	13	13	14	15	—
St. Helens	22	22	23	24	26	30	33
Widnes	18	18	17	19	21	24	30
South Shields	11	12	16	16	21	16	16
Hull K.R.	16	14	15	20	16	23	26
Barrow	4	8	9	6	—	—	—
Millom	2	—	—	—	—	—	—

Promotion and relegation would be two up, and two down. The bottom three clubs in Division Two would retire, but they would be eligible for re-election.

On the Crest of ......a Slump! 1902-03

When St. Helens were not in the original Northern League, even the most ardent supporters were pessimistic as to the future. The inclusion of the Saints into the charmed circle of the League, albeit by the backdoor was therefore, most welcome. Everyone looked forward to a season in which the club would regain its old time position in the football World — even though the road might prove a difficult one.

The current mood of optimism was certainly shared by the club officials. Mr. J. Garner had been elected Chairman of the Committee, with Walter Holland as Treasurer. Most significant of all was the intention of Mr. J. H. Houghton, the previous year's President of the Northern Union, to continue with the secretarial duties.

Other off-the-field developments for 1902-03 included a change of head-quarters to the Talbot Hotel further down Duke Street. The club was now well set up with excellent dressing and committee rooms, although players would still have to be conveyed to the ground by waggonette.

The practice matches had revealed some talented players for the future. It was to be very much a period of transition, especially in the three-quarters. Youngsters such as Charlie Creevey and Tommy Barton were showing great promise, but would need time. Hopes of success were pinned on the experienced shoulders of forwards like Briers, Whiteley, Thompson and Carney. The side was to be led once again by the old warhorse, Tom Foulkes.

Before the opening match of the season against Bradford, the St. Helens Newspaper made the following assessment of the Saints' chances of success:—

"Never perhaps did the St. Helens R. F. C. stand on the threshold of a season in which the prospects are so promising as at the present time".

They did have a tendency to let the heart rule the head in those days. It proved to be a veritable kiss of death. Saints lost to Bradford and managed to lose the next two matches before winning at Brighouse.

Life in the top flight was tough as the side struggled for consistency, but they were soon to find it. Unfortunately, it was of the wrong kind! In a disastrous mid-season slump they lost six games on the trot up to the New Year's Day win over Batley. A further five consecutive defeats were halted only by an unexpected 6 - 3 cup win over Warrington on 14th February.

It provided that great character Cuthbert Pennington with one of his most amusing anecdotes. On paper, Saints were certain to lose, yet once they got their noses in front 'Cuddy' and the forwards played their own game to such purpose that Warrington were defeated.

At half-time Cuddy, who was playing at scrum half asked Tom Foulkes "can I play my own game this half?". "Tha can play what tha likes so long as we win" his captain replied. So the Saints forwards kept on heeling and Cuddy kept kicking the ball out of play, or getting tackled in possession. The ball was kept tight, until the game was won. By all accounts, it was the players turn to get tight afterwards!

The hangover was to continue a week later as Rochdale ended cup hopes for another year. As the season drew to a close, there seemed little prospect of any improvement in league form. Relegation was made certain after Hull Kingston Rovers won easily at Knowsley Road in early April. The Committee had dropped Tom Foulkes for this game. He had looked a shadow of his former self on numerous occasions during the season. The

The Yo-Yo Saints (1902 — 1906)

newspapers argued that such a step should have been taken much earlier on and, by the same token, were not exactly full of praise for his replacement — Wearing.

Predictably, Tommy was reinstated as Saints set out to win their last two games to avoid bottom place in the division. The pressure was off now and they proved there was still some football left in them by travelling to Wigan's new ground at Central Park and winning by five points to three. The Red, Amber and Blacks' triumph over Widnes at a sparsely populated Knowsley Road seven days later left Brighouse in possession of the wooden spoon.

A look at some of the statistics reveals the depressing nature of the season:—

- 10 wins from 36 matches, including one in the Northern Union Cup
- Never scored more than ten points in a winning margin
- Out of 36 matches, 21 tries scored, 20 matches were 'tryless'
- Played at Runcorn on 7th February with 14 men
- Biggest defeat margin v Broughton (A) 0 - 23
- Biggest winning margin v Widnes (H) 8 - 3
- W. Briers led the scorers with 5 tries
- T. Hall kicked 16 goals

Back Where They Belong — 1903-04

Far from being disheartened, the Committee were confident of a quick return to the first division. Secretary Houghton reported that season ticket sales had been brisk and — even more important, the players had stuck loyally by their club. Saints were to meet first division opponents in the re-vamped South West Lancashire League, which consisted of six clubs, St. Helens, Wigan, Widnes, Runcorn, Leigh and Warrington.

Each club was to play five games, a win counting four points, a draw two points, with both sides having an equal share of the gate. Joe Houghton had arranged very favourable dates for the St. Helens games in this competition, four out of the five games were to be played on Bank Holidays. The match at Wigan on Christmas Day drew a record ten thousand plus crowd at Central Park. Considering there were no home matches, St. Helens' results were quite creditable:—

1st September	v	Leigh	Won	5 - 2
Christmas Day	v	Wigan	Lost	6 - 12
New Year's Day	v	Warrington	Lost	3 - 19
Good Friday	v	Widnes	Won	8 - 4
Easter Monday	v	Runcorn	Draw	3 - 3

The road to second division success would be a rocky one however. The Yorkshire fraternity, no doubt disgusted at the prospect of an expensive trip over the Pennines to Knowsley Road, did not exactly extend the olive branch of friendship. Normanton had to post warning notices on their ground after their volatile followers greeted the Saints with a hail of stones. Yorkshire referees could be just as bad, and one official ignored numerous glaring cases of deliberate kicking in the match at Holbeck. The St. Helens Newspaper offered the following advice:—

> *"Saints should be prepared to play the game as Yorkshiremen play it ......and be prepared to rough it if necessary".*

The fun was not just restricted to the White Rose Shire. When Saints travelled to Lancaster on Boxing Day, someone had not done his homework. They became stranded at Preston as the connecting trains to Lancaster had been knocked off for the holidays. This necessitated the charter of a special train which cost the club an extra nine pounds, and made them late into the bargain. The players had to change in the train and rush off to the field.

There was no appointed referee when they got there, and the rulings of the stand-in official had much to do with the homesters' shock victory. Captain Briers thought several times about taking his men off the field, but relented. Pointless and penniless, the dejected Saints boarded their train back to Preston and home.

A few weeks later, Joe Houghton received an anonymous tip-off that one Lancaster player had broken the work clause. After duly consulting his railway time-tables, he travelled more than two hundred miles in search of further evidence. A case was later prepared for the Northern Union General Committee. Lancaster were subsequently fined two guineas, the player — Woodhouse, suspended for nearly a year — and the game replayed. There would be only one winner this time!

Three clubs vied for the two promotion places for most of the season — Wakefield, Holbeck and St. Helens. The Saints were unbeatable at Knowsley Road, but their form away from home had been disappointing. Gradually, Wakefield drew away from the pack to leave a two-horse race between St. Helens and Holbeck, for second place.

Before the last Saturday of the season, the league looked like this:—

		P	W	D	L	Pts
1.	Wakefield	31	26	1	4	53
2.	Holbeck	31	24	1	6	49
3.	St. Helens	31	21	5	5	47

The final act of the drama was about to take place. Holbeck lost their last match at Barrow. Saints almost shoved poor old South Shields into the nearby Leg o'Mutton Dam — winning by 23 - 0.

St. Helens and Holbeck had thus tied for second place, and a play-off was necessary to decide which club would be promoted with Wakefield. The season had officially ended and the Northern Rugby League had to apply to

The Yo-Yo Saints (1902 — 1906)

the Northern Union for permission to play the game. It was decided that the 'Test Match' could take place at Huddersfield on Saturday, 14th May.

"War on Foreign Soil" the local newspapers called it, as a couple of hundred 'Sintelliners' made their way to Fartown. They were in confident mood, despite the absence of Kitty Briers — stricken with Diphtheria. Their trip was made worthwhile when Charlie Creevey streaked through the desperate Holbeck defence to score the winning try. He had been laid low himself before Christmas with a serious bout of pneumonia.

Kitty was a popular fellow and he was not forgotten. Club officials sent him telegrams at the interval and at the finish, which were very welcome. An enthusiastic crowd greeted the team back in St. Helens, where they then boarded a waggonette direct to Briers' Thatto Heath home, reporting progress in three cheers!

Ironically, Holbeck's most successful season was also to be their last. Soon afterwards they sold their ground to Leeds City AFC — which later became Leeds United. Decades later, soccer players who felt the ferocity of a Norman Hunter tackle had good reason to curse those Saints of 1904!

Tommy Foulkes — Local Superstar

On 23rd April, 1904 — St. Helens thrashed Lancaster 36 - 2 at Knowsley Road in front of a large crowd. The match had been set apart for the benefit of Tommy Foulkes, the veteran full-back who was to retire at the end of the season after fifteen years service to the club.

Foulkes began with St. Helens in 1889-90, the last season at the old ground in Dentons Green. His previous experience of football was with Ravenhead St. Johns as a half-back for a few years. At the end of 1888-89, he competed in a works competition match at Dentons Green. The Saints officials liked what they saw and signed him on the spot. Despite breaking both wrists in his first season, a start which would have ended many players career, he settled down to become one of the finest full-backs in the North of England.

County honours soon followed and he represented Lancashire on eleven occasions, ten under the Rugby Union. He was on the losing side twice, both against Yorkshire.

For seven out of his fifteen seasons, from 1896-7, he was club captain. His first season as skipper was a memorable one as Saints reached the Challenge Cup final against Batley. Yet he remained scathing of one or two of his players that day. "If they had all been triers" he maintained "we would have taken that cup back home with us".

When he relinquished the captaincy, it was his dearest wish that the position be handed to his old chum Kitty Briers. This the Committee did without question.

The Yo-Yo Saints (1902 — 1906)

Tommy's fearless, dashing style, endeared him to the Saints supporters, and he repaid them with unswerving loyalty — despite offers from elsewhere. In the early part of his career in the so-called amateur days, he made a few appearances for the crack Oldham club. In the dressing room after one game he found a sovereign in each boot, together with an invitation to go for a slap-up meal in a posh Manchester hotel.

Such inducements proved most attractive to young Foulkes, especially when they offered him a job to go with a place in their team. He decided he would throw in his lot with the Rough'yeds, and went to Shaw street station with his luggage to catch the train for Oldham. Although he was sorely tempted, the money was not everything. The prospect of leaving his close pals Kitty Briers and Ned Ashcroft did not appeal to him that much. He promptly returned home, unpacked his bags and asked for his job back at Cannington-Shaws bottleworks, where he was an apprentice sorter. That was Tommy Foulkes, a St. Helens man through and through!

A Perilous Existence

Saints promotion into the first division for 1904-05 proved disastrous. Results showed they were just not good enough for the top flight. Shortly after Christmas, the Committee decided to give an extra bonus of five shillings to each first team player who played in every match won, to the end of the season. This rare inducement hardly stretched the club's already ailing finances!

Nine successive defeats from early February to the end of April sealed their fate. They finished seventeenth out of eighteen clubs. Runcorn were the wooden spoonists.

Relegation was not inevitable however. It was becoming obvious that a change in the leagues would take place once again. The finances of many second division clubs had deteriorated alarmingly. When put to the vote, it was decided to form one major league — a motion no doubt fully endorsed by the relieved St. Helens representatives! Clubs from the same county were to play each other and arrange inter-county fixtures, with positions decided on a percentage basis.

In today's two-division football, with three-up, three-down — it is not uncommon for the weaker promoted clubs to make a quick return to the second division. Fulham and Whitehaven are recent teams who have much in common with those Saints of yesteryear — the original yo-yo team of Rugby League.

Pocket Nook Boys

In the early nineteen hundreds — Banks and Hall were making a name for themselves in St. Helens. Although sounding like music hall comedians, this dynamic duo performed on the rugby field as Saints' regular half-back pairing for several years. Tommy Hall in particular, was notable for his skill in dropping goals.

During one match at Knowsley Road, Saints were pressing and a scrum was formed near the posts. The ball squirted out very quickly while the referee had his head turned away. In a flash, Hall dropped the ball to his boot and banged it over the bar. The referee's attention had only lapsed for a split second — but it was enough for Hall's brilliance.

When the referee again turned his eyes to the scrum, the forwards were still struggling, apparently not knowing the ball had left. The referee wondered where it had gone as well, but the crowed yelled its approval of the goal. Hall told him he had dropped the goal and the touch judge verified it. The referee allowed a goal he had never even seen!

It was a tough game in those days, especially for half-backs. Broken limbs could mean financial disaster for an unlucky player. There was no insurance to fall back on. Little wonder that Pearsons Weekly was the best read paper of its day among the rugby-playing fraternity. They had to fill in the coupon in Pearsons to be sure of six weeks insurance in case of injury. "Have you signed your Pearsons yet?" — was a familiar question on match days. Anyone who hadn't promptly did so.

The Cinder Field

Banks and Hall were from Pocket Nook, and graduates of the premier junior club for miles around — known as the St. Helens Shamrocks. They learned their football on a area of flattened cinders from the nearby gas works, known appropriately as the Cinder Field.

Many great players have joined the Saints after an early 'breaking-in' on the Cinder Field, now alas covered over by a council house estate. David Traynor, a cup finalist in 1897 for Saints — was born in that area. Others include Billy Lavin, Tommy Gormley a Recs-Saint, Teddy Toole, Frank Mooney and the famous Creevey brothers.

The Sporting Creeveys

The Creeveys — orginally hawkers in the fish trade, can quite rightly claim to be Pocket Nook's most famous sporting family. Brothers Charlie, Jimmy and Matt Creevey all played for Saints at some stage in their careers, after starring for the Shamrocks. Indeed, all three played against the visiting All Blacks in 1907, when Jimmy Creevey had the honour of captaining the St. Helens side.

The brothers were born competitors, products of an age when you had to make your own entertainment. In their youth they would play endless games of football; wall tennis on the nearest gable end; have swimming competitions in the canal; race bicycles on the Cinder Field, or play bowls with oranges bought from the local grocers.

Born in 1888, Matt Creevey was the most gifted athlete of them all. A devastating half-back, he possessed a brilliant burst of speed, a blinding dummy and a simultaneous sidestep. His other priceless asset was the ability to change his position to take his pass at different angles while playing at stand-off half.

Matt was also the undefeated World champion standing jumper, with a staggering personal best of 14' 2". He used to jump with a ten pound weight in each hand. These used to be thrown backwards whilst in mid-air to give extra lift.

He could jump over the average man's head, onto a horse's back and off again in one movement, into a fair sized barrel and out again in the same way and jump backwards over six ordinary chairs. At one time he travelled the music halls performing jumping feats as the 'Human Panther'. When the first World War broke out, he was about to embark on a World tour — including the United States of America. Several years before, however, he was transferred to Warrington — who allegedly paid a sizeable fee for his signature. At the end of one particular training session, he was challenged to a 'best of three' sprints by the legendary Warrington flyer — Jack Fish.

Creevey won the first race with consummate ease, and toyed with is opponent in the second. "Has anyone told tee tha' can run?" gasped a startled Jack Fish afterwards, "tha wants to throw yon jumping weights in t'cut· (Canal) and get measured for some pumps".

Matt was well aware of his blistering pace. Some years later, while playing at Salford, he was approached by a Manchester bookmaker — Moses Tarsh, about competing in the prestigious Salford Borough Sprint. The event was held on 26th December, 1916 — and Matt won the £100 first prize. Tarsh, several thousand pounds better off as a result, gave Matt a commemorative gold watch bearing the following inscription:—

"Presented as a token of friendship, Mo to Matt, 26th December, 1916".

Matt was also well-known in St. Helens as landlord of the Red Lion in Vernon Street, and the Canal Vaults near Pilkingtons Sheet Works in Canal Street. His nephew, Charlie Creevey, used to carry his bag for him when he went training for rugby, sprints or some of his amazing jumping feats. He is in no doubt as to his uncle's rare athletic prowess:—

"Today's players would have been looking at his heels when he'd gone. He proved it with his professional sprinting — that's enough. How many men could go out any night of the week and do even time? (Seventy yards in seven seconds). He was always in good condition. When he had a first-class preparation for jumping or running, they took him away from Auntie Kitty and the kids for six weeks at a time. Those old timers never did things by half".

Unlucky for Some

At the Northern Union AGM in the close season of 1906, many clubs pressed for the reduction in the number of players in a side. St. Helens proposed the dropping of one player, Whitehaven Recreation three. Warrington — supported by Leigh, suggested a compromise of 13-a-side. The proposal was carried by forty-three votes to eighteen. For the sake of open football, two of the forwards would disappear. Saints were not too despondent. After all, it was estimated that this would save each club about a hundred pounds a year in wages!

Another major innovation was a top four play-off to decide the championship. The top club played the fourth and the second met the third, with the higher placed club having ground advantage. The final was to be held at a neutral venue.

This was pie-in-the-sky for the sad Saints. Since their reprieve from the second division status at the end of 1904-05, results had been depressing to say the least. The Committee always lacked the money to sign top quality players, and so put their faith in local talent.

The policy did provide some success however. On New Year's Day 1906, forward Frank Lee and highly promising full-back Tommy Barton became the club's first representatives at international level. They appeared for England against the Other Nationalities at Wigan in a three-all draw. Barton might well have been lost to rugby. A brick-setter by trade, he spent some time in America in the early 1900's, cashing in on the building boom — and even played gridiron football for a spell!

Matters Arising — Assorted entries from the Minute Book of the Saints Committee, 1903-06

23.11.03 — 2,000 hand bills to be printed and two sandwich men engaged for Wakefield Trinity match.

14. 3.04 — Application read from Hurling Club to rent football ground during summer months — not entertained.

16. 8.04 — Resolved — that S. Sherwood be 'signed on'. Terms agreed 'Suit of clothes and 30/-'.

30. 9.04 — Resolved — that fifteen or eighteen pairs of galoshes be purchased for team practising.

6.12.04 — Resolved — that Mr. F. Turner be objected to as an official in any of our future matches.

28. 3.05 — The Secretary was instructed to write to the Chief Constable re: gambling etc. on football ground on Sundays.

The Yo-Yo Saints (1902 – 1906)

21. 8.05 — Resolved — that we accept the tender of the St. Helens Carriage Company for supply of waggonette and cab from and to Station and ground via Headquarters at 12/6 and 4/- respectively per match.

13.11.05 — No schoolboys or youths match be played on the ground unless someone is in charge of the boys who go up as spectators, such persons to be responsible for any damage done.

— That the groundsman be instructed not to loan keys to players, without authority.

18.12.05 — Resolved — that six Policemen be engaged for Runcorn and Wigan matches.

— That Treasurer engage extra cab for conveyance of money after the above matches.

12. 2.06 — Resolved — that .... be suspended over Saturday, and threatened with legal proceedings unless he makes a clean breast of the theft of the timber from the ground.

— That S. Johnson be written to, to the effect that his work in the scrimmages is not satisfactory.

17. 9.06 — Resolved — that the club's colours be registered as red, amber and black. That eighteen red, amber and black jerseys, twelve pairs of pants (at usual price), twelve pairs of hose and two elastic knee bandages be ordered.

29.10.06 — Bills be posted on the ground requesting better behaviour on the ground by spectators.

Chapter 4

The Colonial Saints (1907 – 1914)

All Blacks or All Golds?

When Freddie Ah Kuoi led the tenth Kiwi Tourists on to the Knowsley Road turf in October, 1980 he was continuing a tradition begun by his rugby forefathers over seventy years ago. It was in 1907-08 that the newly formed professional New Zealand international team visited Britain for the first time. They were managed by a twenty-four year old post office clerk from Wellington – Albert Henry Baskerville, and had no previous experience of rugby in the Northern Union.

Soon after settling into their headquarters at the Grand Central Hotel in Leeds, they were given lectures on the rules by J. H. Smith, a leading referee. The tour caused uproar in New Zealand, where professionalism was a dirty word. In London, their Agent General expressed the opinion that the 'All Golds' as they were called, would bring no credit to their country.

Despite the lack of official support and their inexperience of the new code, results went well. The long awaited visit to Knowsley Road took place on Wednesday 30th October, 1907 – in front of an estimated 8,000 crowd who were not in the least deterred by the persistent drizzle.

Spectators could purchase a match programe on card for a penny, which contained the words of the 'Famous Maori War Cry' for the uninitiated Lancastrians.

The All Black team – containing some famous names, was listed in an unusual way with two five-eighths, W. Wynyard and Lance Todd. Yet it was an Australian who was the main attraction. Herbert 'Dally' Messenger – a fast, clever three-quarter had played magnificently for Australia in three matches against the paid All Blacks in Sydney shortly before the tour began. Baskerville was naturally delighted when he decided to accompany the party to Britain.

There was a tremendous buzz of anticipation as 'Bumper' Wright and his men ran on to the field swearing death to the Saints with their blood curdling war cry. At 3.30 p.m. precisely, Councillor Norman Pilkington kicked off for the Colonials, and the fun began.

The early exchanges were fierce as the rival packs vied for supremacy. Jack Manchester, the St. Helens winger, had an excellent chance of opening the home account when he brushed off Messenger and streaked for the line only to lose possession at the vital moment. Jum Turtill, the New Zealand full-back stopped a forward rush and fed his three-quarters. 'Tracker' Lavery kicked over the defence, caught the ball and raced in for the opening try which Messenger converted.

On restarting, the Saints attacked like demons — and it was not long before they got back on level terms. A splendid round of passing by the home backs left Charlie Creevey with just enough room to ground the leather and Knowsley Road erupted a second time as he magnificently converted his own try from the most difficult of angles.

Five all — and Saints piled on the pressure. Excitement reached fever pitch when Charlie once again out-paced his opponents. He had only Jum Turtill to face but, once again, the full-back showed his class by hurling the ex-Shamrock into touch by the corner flag.

It was now the New Zealanders' turn to put the pressure on, with immediate results. From a scrum near the Saints line, W. Wynyard fed winger Smith who raced away for a grand score. Messenger again converted 10 – 5.

Official Programme for All Blacks game

Even though the All Blacks had the lead when the second half began, they started to look shaky under intense St. Helens pressure. It was time for Messenger's magic to turn the tables. The St. Helens Reporter describes the incident as follows:—

"Saints attacked in the visitors' 25 where Messenger got hold, and put in a neat punt; the ball appeared to be going well into touch, but he

A fine body of men! St. Helens Rangers in their black jerseys and long breeches strike a splendid pose outside the old Abbey Hotel circa 1882/83. Captain Alec Borthwick sits proudly on the right. 'Monsey' Parr is second from the right on the back row.
(Photo courtesy Mrs. Weston)

Lancashire v Rest of England 1888
Saints' Skipper Billy Cross is second from the right, on the grass. Jimmy Pyke of the Recs — the town's first rugby international is third from the right on the back row.
(Photo courtesy T. Webb)

Two Saints' Captains featured on cigarette cards of the 1880's —
Alec Borthwick (left) and Billy Cross.
(Courtesy C. Johnstone)

Bob Doherty's splendid blue velvet Club Cap —
awarded in 1889 — and still in pristine condition today.
(Courtesy G. Doherty)

Proud to be Saints!

Billy Cross and the Lads wearing their blue and white striped jerseys in front of the dressing hut at Knowsley Road circa 1894/95. Back row l to r:– Mr. T. C. Wilcock (Chairman), J. Appleton, E. Ashcroft, W. Whiteley, J. Brownbill, W. Wilson, J. Gladwin, T. Sudlow, J. Edwards (Official). Front row:– P. Dale, W. Cross, Jones, Graham. Boy Mascot:– J. Garrity. Middle row seated:– T. Foulkes, R. Doherty, F. Little, Rennie.

(Photo courtesy St. Helens Library)

The superb gold medal presented to Saints' forward 'Ned' Ashcroft for winning the Lancashire Second Division Championship in 1893/94.

(Courtesy A. Roby)

In Search of Cup Glory 1897

The two antagonists line up for the camera with a sea of Headingley faces in the background. On the left, the Batleyites look determined to uphold the pride of the White Rose County. The superstitious Saints, with their lucky old jerseys and unsettled mascot seem unconcerned with events.

(Photo courtesy Bagshaw Museum, Batley)

David 'Red' Traynor, Saints' try scorer in the 1897 Cup Final seen here in his Lancashire jersey and Cap.
(Photo courtesy Mrs. Kenrick)

Mighty Millom 1904/05

A young Fred Trenwith, Saints' 'Human Torpedo' sits on the far right of the front row.

The Saints line up outside their somewhat draughty dressing rooms at the Talbot Hotel before the match against Wigan on 9th March, 1907.
St. Helens beat the Riversiders 10 – 8.

Back Row l to r (Players only):—
Smith, F. Mooney, J. Pope, W. Briers, W. Whiteley, J. Mavitty.

Seated l to r:—
J. Creevey, T. Barton (Capt.), J. Hillen, C. Creevey.

On Ground l to r:—
J. Atkinson, M. Creevey, E. Toole.

(Photo courtesy Mrs. Skepper)

Ready for the Fray

Thirteen red amber and black Saints, plus reserve, line up before the league match with Warrington on September 28th, 1907. St. Helens won a magnificent game 7 –6, one of only seven victories enjoyed by them during the 1907/08 season! Hillen scored a try and Charlie Creevey two goals.

Back row l to r:—
Smith, Appleton (Trainers); Matt Creevey — one of the fastest half-backs off the mark ever seen, world champion jumper and 70 yards sprint champion; W. Mercer - occasional pack member; Jim Mavitty — county forward, star swimmer and one of the strongest men for his size seen in a Saints' jersey; Jack Pope — hooker; Bill Whiteley (Reserve) — last of the original North Countrymen; W. J. 'Gillie' Hillen — a tough Cumbrian centre; Sgt. Major Hannaford (Committee).

Middle row l to r:—
Frank Mooney — a forward from Pocket Nook; Jim 'Butcher' Prescott — a rough and ready Lancashire forward; Jimmy Creevey — Skipper and left centre threequarter; brother Charlie sits next to him — strong, fast and a regular goal kicker; J. Bate — understudy for regular wing flyer Jack Manchester.

Front row l to r:—
'Kitty' Briers — the best dribbling forward the Saints ever had — one of the quickest, too; Frank Drake — signed from Salford the previous week — set to debut at scrum-half; Teddy Toole — full-back or scrum-half completes the Pocket Nook connection.

(Photo courtesy St. Helens Library)

The 1907/08 All-Blacks

(1) Cross, (2) Todd, (3) Rowe, (4) Mackrell, (5) McGregor, (6) Wright, (7) E. N. Smith, (8) Wrigley, (9) Messenger, (10) Trevarthen, (11) Johnson, (12) Baskerville, (13) Lavery, (14) Kelly, (15) Callam, (16) Byrne, (17) W. Wynyard, (18) T. H. Smith, (19) Hodgson, (20) Turtill, (21) Tyler, (22) Dunning, (23) Tyne, (24) Gilchrist, (25) Lile, (26) J. Wynyard, (27) Fraser, (36) Pearce.

Two players, Kelly (14) and Turtill (20) later signed for Saints.
Edgar Wrigley (8) was coach at Knowsley Road for a spell in the 1920's.

The little ivy-covered cottage at Eccleston Hill, an essential place of pilgrimage for the early Colonial tourists. (Photo courtesy St. Helens Library)

*Little Arthur Kelly, the former All-Black scrum-half — Saints first ever Colonial signing in 1908.
(Courtesy C. Johnstone)*

A Saints 'Superstar' before the First World War! Tommy Barton wearing his England Cap from 1905/06.

Spot the Phantom Tourist!

Tommy Barton (top left) on a photograph to commemorate the 1910 Northern Union Touring team to Australia and New Zealand. (Photo courtesy C. Potter)

Saints' 'Flying Curate' — the Rev. C. M. Chavasse during his days at Oxford University.

(Photo courtesy L. M. Foster-Carter)

Past and Present

Fred Trenwith's Lancashire jersey from 1912, worn by Saints' scrum-half Neil Holding, himself a County player.

(Courtesy Mrs. Oscer)

All in a Good Cause!

*Turtill's Toddlers line up in the Saints' blue and black jerseys, complete with 'Teddy Bear' mascot.
Back row l to r:— Albert Smith, Walter Norbury, Harry Mercer, Tom Topping, B. Ireland, Willie Slater, George Howarth, Charlie Glover (Trainer).
Middle row l to r:— P. Fildes, H. Kerr, Harry Johnson, W. Elliot, F. Beards, Jum Turtill (with young son, Alan).
Front row l to r:— Jim May, H. Saunders, Percy Jeffrey.
(Photo courtesy J. Halligan)*

A Fine Memento!

Jack Potter's Runner's-up medal from the 1920 St. Helens R.F.C. Medal Competition. The team — Glover's Own.

(Courtesy C. Potter)

The Colonial Saints (1907 — 1914)

gathered it with great cleverness and, speeding on like a stag, scored a great try which the crowd applauded to the echo".

In another raid by the visitors, Saints full-back Atkinson tried desperately to clear his lines, but managed to kick the ball practically over his own head. Smith gleefully scampered in to collect try number four. Two further tries ensured a 24-5 victory for the All Blacks, yet despite the score — the match had been fairly even. The large crowd certainly enjoyed themselves, and warmly applauded both sides off the field.

Clad in their narrow rimmed straw hats emblazoned with the silver fern, the Colonials were a popular side — both on and off the field. The St. Helens public took them to their hearts. It was very much a mutual attraction, as the New Zealanders felt more at home in St. Helens than anywhere else on tour. There was certainly a strong link with their own country, as Richard Seddon — the popular New Zealand Prime Minister from 1893-1906 was a St. Helens man. During their stay, the players made a pilgrimage to his birthplace and were photographed outside the cottage half-way up Eccleston Hill, which stands to this day.

DETAILS OF NEW ZEALAND 'ALL GOLDS' VERSUS ST. HELENS
Wednesday, 30th October, 1907

Name	Nickname	Age	Height	Weight
H. S. Turtill	'JUM'	27	5' 9"	11.05
J. A. Lavery	'TRACKER'	27	5' 11"	12.07
G. W. Smith (V.Capt.)	'SMITHY'	34	5' 7"	12.02
H. H. Messenger	'DALLY'	24	5' 8"	12.00
L. B. Todd	'TODDIE'	24	5' 7"	10.00
W. T. Wynyard	'CORK'	25	5' 9"	11.03
J. R. Wynyard	'DICKIE'	22	5' 8"	11.10
W. Johnson	'MASSA'	25	6' 1"	13.08
C. J. Pearce	'CARLO'	25	5' 10"	14.05
H. R. Wright (Capt.)	'BUMPER'	23	5' 11"	13.08
A. Lyle	'FATTY'	21	5' 11"	14.00
T. W. Cross	'ANGRY'	29	6' 0"	14.07
D. Gilchrist	'NED'	23	5' 11"	13.03

NEW ZEALAND TOUR — 1907-08
Wednesday, 30th October, 1907
ST. HELENS (5)5   NEW ZEALAND (10)24

ST. HELENS: J. Atkinson, C. Creevey, J. Creevey (Capt.) 1T, 1G, W. Hillen, J. Manchester, M. Creevey, E. Toole, W. Briers, J. Pope, J. Mavitty, F. Mooney, J. Bradburn, Smith.

The Colonial Saints (1907 — 1914)

NEW ZEALAND: H. S. Turtill, H. Messenger 1T 3G, G. Smith 2T, J. Lavery 1T, L. B. Todd, W. Wynyard 1T, R. Wynyard, D. Gilchrist, T. Cross, A. Lyle, H. Wright (Capt.) 1T, C. Pearce, W. Johnson.

Referee: Mr. Tonge (Swinton)
Attendance: 8,000

St. Helens re-visited

The All Blacks enjoyed themselves so much that they returned in the New Year to play a second match at Knowsley Road, and revisited the many friends they had made in the town. During the week of their visit Saints Secretary Harry Mercer organized a whist drive and dance at the Town Hall. Tickets cost half-a-crown for gents, two shillings for ladies. Double tickets proved popular at five bob each.

Two New Zealanders, Kelly and skipper Wright, were present at the function. Later in the evening 'Bumper' had the honour of presenting 'Kitty' Briers with a cheque for £19.15s.5d. This included the proceeds of his benefit match against Widnes, and the Shilling Testimonial Fund in the St. Helens Newspaper. As the popular Saint rose to receive the gift, the band struck up 'Auld Lang Syne'. Briers then thanked the people who had contributed to the success of his benefit. Everyone agreed it had been fully deserved!

By a strange coincidence the return game was another wash out in the weather sense. Strong winds and heavy rain kept the attendance down to 3,000 — yet play was always open and interesting for the faithful few. Appearing for the All Blacks for the first time on tour was Albert Baskerville, no mean player in his own right. Only his secretarial duties had prevented him from playing in other matches.

Wynyard kicked off for the visitors against the gale and it was not long before the home side took full advantage. Manchester scored after a forward rush, as Turtill waited in vain to kick dead. Saints kept up the pressure, and play was restricted to the New Zealand quarter of the field.

After further forward pressure Frank Lee picked up and dashed over the line. Jimmy Creevey added a neat conversion. Immediately afterwards, the same player made a tactical left foot drop across the field towards Manchester. To everyone's delight, the wind completely turned the course of the ball and carried it through the posts.

The ten point advantage did not last long after half-time. 'Maori' Tyler opened the visitors' account with a splendid touchdown. Shortly after, scrum half Wynyard scored two almost identical tries from around the base of the scrum. Messenger converted the second to give the Colonials the lead. Towards the end of the game there were great cheers as Baskerville expertly collected a cross-kick and crashed over to score near the posts. Messenger duly converted. It was a fine epitaph for 'Baski' who was to die tragically of pneumonia in Austrialia on the last leg of the tour.

'Massa' Johnson completed the scoring to set the scene on another delightful exhibiton of New Zealand Rugby.

The following day, both sets of players and officials were together again. They joined a packed congregation at Christ Church, Eccleston on the dedication of new choir stalls and a prayer desk. These were placed in the church by the late Right Hon. Richard J. Seddon's widow, in memory of her husband.

Seven days after bidding farewell to the Colonial poineers, Saints fell victim to some more 'All Black' magic at the home of Whitehaven Recreation. The non-leaguers sensationally knocked them out of the Challenge Cup. By a strange irony, the first round draw had been made by a visiting celebrity — New Zealand skipper 'Bumper' Wright. Just as well he had departed!

NEW ZEALAND TOUR 1907-08 — RETURN FIXTURE
Saturday, 22nd February, 1908
At Knowsley Road
ST. HELENS (10)10   NEW ZEALAND (0)21

ST. HELENS: J. Atkinson, J. Creevey (Capt.) 2G, J. Evans, W. Hillen, J. Manchester 1T, M. Creevey, F. Trenwith, W. Briers, F. Lee 1T, J. Pope, Holmes, W. Wharton, J. Mavitty.

NEW ZEALAND: Turtill, Messenger 3G, Howe, Tyne, Wrigley, Tyler 1T, R. Wynyard 2T, Wright (Capt.), Johnson 1T, Pearce, Baskerville 1T, Dunning, Trevarthen.

Referee: Mr. Priestley (Salford)
Attendance: 3,000

Saints sign a 'Baskerville Boy'

The New Zealanders dashing style of football brought them a whole host of admirers and, not surprisingly, several members of the touring side were recruited by the Northern Union clubs. George Smith joined Oldham, Edgar Wrigley went to Huddersfield, while Wigan secured the services of Lance Todd and 'Massa' Johnson.

In December, 1908 — Arthur Kelly, the dapper scrum-half from Petone, Wellington became Saints' first colonial import. The Knowsley Road faithful gave a warm greeting to the former All Black as he ran out for his debut against Rochdale. Unfortunately, the Hornets had a different sort of welcome in store, of the rough-house variety.

Yet little Arthur took the knocks in his stride and came bouncing back for more. He was a daredevil character, who seemed to relish nothing more than a headlong dive on to oncoming forwards' feet in order to stop a dribble. He soon became a firm favourite with supporters.

The Kangaroos Nilled

The Antipodean connection continued in the 1908-09 season with the visit of the first Australians to Britain, complete with a live kangaroo mascot. When acting skipper Messenger led out the Amber and Blues at Knowsley Road on a Wednesday afternoon in early February, the weather once again showed its contempt for the big occasion. The rain poured down as 'Dally' led a weakened team through their fierce Aboriginal war cry in front of a depressingly small gate of only two thousand spectators.

To the delight of those present however, the first half was dominated by St. Helens, who adapted much better to the heavy pitch and greasy ball. Early pressure paid off when centre Harold Greenwood made a perfect opening for 'Butcher' Prescott to crash through and score. Saints' tackling was sharp at this stage, and the Aussies went further behind from a swift counter attack. Jimmy Greenwood charged down an attempted clearance by scrum-half Butler and touched down for try number two.

After half-time, Saints continued to dominate in the mud. Winger Flanagan put the game beyond doubt for the homesters by catching a miskick from 'Alby' Rosenfeld and dashing over for a try.

Talk in the local pubs that night centred around the display of full-back Tommy Barton who played a blinder. He appeared to be the natural successor to Tommy Foulkes, but his attacking powers were such that he was unlikely to remain at full-back all his playing career.

The Saints' Committee were naturally delighted with the result, yet takings from the match were poor and did not even amount to the Australians' guarantee figure of £50. Disgruntled club officials were faced with a near forty pound loss from the proceedings.

The Australians were not without their problems too. They left for home on 10th March, 1909 short of four players who had signed on for English clubs, and the unfortunate kangaroo — which had died the day before. It was said that the English weather had been too much for it. The visit to St. Helens would have done little to improve the ailing marsupial's health!

AUSTRALIAN TOUR 1908-09
Wednesday, 10th February, 1909
ST. HELENS (6)9   AUSTRALIA (0)0

ST. HELENS: T. Barton,   J. Flanagan 1T,   J. Greenwood 1T, H. Greenwood, Harris, R. Hill, F. Trenwith, W. Briers (Capt.), Bradley, E. Helsby, J. Prescot 1T, J. Pope, S. Johnson.

The Colonial Saints (1907 — 1914)

AUSTRALIA: C. Hedley, D. Frawley, W. Heidke, H. Messenger (Capt.), A. Morton, A. Rosenfeld, A. Butler, E. Courtney, R. Graves, S. Pearce, J. Abercrombie, P. Moir, W. Cann.

Referee: Mr. Smith (Widnes)
Attendance: 1,500

The Coming of Turtill

On 23rd June, 1984 — Britain failed in their bid to capture the Ashes after defeat in the second test match at Lang Park, Brisbane. St. Helens supporters, however, received a most welcome consolation present after the game when Mal Meninga, the giant Australian centre, became a Saint for the 1984-85 season.

The Brisbane Policeman had made his name with the unbeaten 1982 kangaroo tourists to Britain, with a record tally for Anglo-Australian tests of 21 goals and 48 points — just the type of player to rocket the club back into the limelight as one of Rugby League's top teams.

Yet this is a case of history repeating itself. Almost seventy-five years ago to the day, Saints officials were involved in talks with another famous Colonial player who — they hoped, would transform the club's fortunes.

Hubert Sydney Turtill was born in London, but as an infant went to New Zealand with his parents in 1884. A chubby youngster who was nicknamed 'Jumbo' by the passengers travelling with his family on the ship out, shortened to 'Jum' — this name remained with him for the rest of his life.

Jum Turtill had gained a fearsome reputation on the All Blacks' tour of 1907-08. In the opinion of many who saw him he was the World's best full-back. He could kick well with either foot, and was gifted with tremendous tackling power and a fine turn of speed.

He later returned to England with his wife, a New Zealand lady, for the purpose of signing for Salford — and was induced to sign for the Saints before Salford knew it. It was a great surprise, especially as the club was one of the league's poorer relations, but Turtill wanted to settle down in St. Helens. He had made friends in the town during the tour. His old chum

The Colonial Saints (1907 – 1914)

Arthur Kelly had signed for the Saints some months before. When the club ensured him remunerative employment as a traveller for a local firm, together with a £150 signing-on fee, the rest was easy.

Turtill's signing was big news in Northern Union circles that week. The St. Helens Newspaper praised the move and hinted at a new era of success for the club:—

"The signing of Turtill is convincing proof of the determination of the Saints' Committee to have a team for the coming season that will hold its own with the best".

Golden Years

This mood of optimism proved to be thoroughly justified. 1909-10 saw the Saints come to the fore as one of the most attractive teams in the Northern Union. Although a trophy once again eluded them, their fast open style of play pushed them into tenth place in the table. It was the beginning of a period when the game was to reach a popularity in the town which has rarely been equalled.

The back division of the club was particularly strong. Jum Turtill an ever-present, was a sensation in his first season. He added a whole new dimension to full-back play with his attacking instincts. Fast, clever and brainy – he was the inspiration of the side. He also completed the first century of points scored by an individual player during one season in the club's history, with 53 goals.

The two wingers, Flanagan and Barton, played soccer in their youth before turning to the handling code, as Alf Ellaby was to do many years later. Jimmy Flanagan scored tries like they were going out of fashion in 1909-10, a total of 31 in 34 appearances. The fair haired flyer also scored four tries in a match twice, and bagged three hat tricks!

Tommy Barton, the captain of the side had been moved to the wing with the arrival of Turtill, but it did not bother him in the slightest. He could play anywhere in the three-quarters with devastating effect. A vivid description of Barton's all-round power was once written by a local pressman:—

"He would leave a trail of dead and dying in his wake. Where he could not swerve or side-step he went straight on, his great strength, speed and determination carrying him through all but the best defences".

Although hampered by injury early on, he stormed back to find his form, scoring fourteen tries in typical style.

Jimmy Greenwood, a fast centre with a beautiful side-step was one of Wigan's few mistakes. they signed him from Hebden Bridge, became disappointed and sold him to St. Helens for a song. St. Helens once sold his partner – Charlie Creevey to Wigan for £200 to keep the club afloat. Two

The Colonial Saints (1907 – 1914)

seasons later he rejoined the Saints and never looked back. Just like 'Red' Traynor and Bob Doc years before, Creevey would flash round Tom Barton and dart down the wing with a suddenness that took his opponents completely by surprise. What would we give for a back division like that today?

Linking them to the pack were Matt Creevey, stand-off half-back and Freddy Trenwith, scrum-half. Trenwith, the iron man, was a little Cumbrian who ended his career on the football field at Leigh, and made a successful come-back the same day. Tom Reynolds, 'Premier' of the St. Helens Newspaper, takes up the story:—

> "He was badly thrown during the match and was carried beneath the stand apparently in a dying condition. A Doctor went down to his aid and the club Chairman went with him. The latter returned a few moments later with the gloomy tidings "Trenwith will never play football again".
>
> Imagine the amazement of the crowd therefore, when not long afterwards a white-faced little figure came trotting out again and took his place on the field. 'Trenny' was not easily killed".

An expert with the Cumberland throw, Trenwith was one of the most accomplished all-round scrum-halves ever to play rugby league. It took two or three men to watch him every match, and Matt Creevey was helped to make a reputation at stand-off all the more easily because Trenwith took so much stopping. Yet Creevey was a law unto himself with his perfect timing of the ball and his lightning leap past an opponent.

There were great characters in the pack too, such as Frank 'Boyler' Lee — St. Helens' first international forward. Jimmy Mavitty, the Cliff Watson of his day, represented his county at swimming as well as football. 'Kitty' Briers retained the links with the old days, still as consistent as ever. Between Mavitty and Briers, Jack Pope — a fine hooker, kept up a steady supply of ball for his three-quarters.

Bradley, Helsby, 'Butcher' Prescott and Micklethwaite — from Dewsbury, made up a pack which could hold its own with the best in the Union. There were others too, at the tail end of the 1910 season, showing form that held out great hopes for the future.

The curtain was brought down on a memorable season with a benefit match for that loyal North Country Forward Bill Whiteley. Jum Turtill assembled a Colonial side to play against the Saints. They came to St. Helens and played at their own expense, such was their respect for the popular full-back. New Zealand winger George Smith said later that they could not refuse such a request.

On the morning of the match came the sad news of the death of Edward VII. Had it been possible, the game would have been postponed, but it was not practicable. Both teams wore black arm bands as a mark of respect.

The Colonial Saints (1907 – 1914)

Billy Cross and Jim Graham acted as touch judges for their old comrade, while 'Boyler' Lee guested for the opposition. Turtill's Colonials were much the better team, and won 24 - 42 in a delightful free-scoring game.

BILL WHITELEY BENEFIT MATCH
Tuesday, 10th May, 1910
At Knowsley Road
ST. HELENS (10)24   TURTILL'S COLONIALS (24)42

ST. HELENS: J. Mosedale, J. Flanagan 3T, J. Greenwood 1T, 2G, E. Toole 1G, J. Manchester 1T, H. Greenwood, M. Creevey, W. Briers, W. Bradley, J. Mavitty, J. Pope 1T, Barnes, S. Daniels.

TURTILL'S COLONIALS: Turtill 3G, Rowe 1T, Smith 1T, Todd 1T, McPhail 2T, Anlezark 1T, Rosenfeld, Seeling 2T, Trevarthen, O'Malley 2T, Lavery 2G, Gray, Lee (St. Helens).

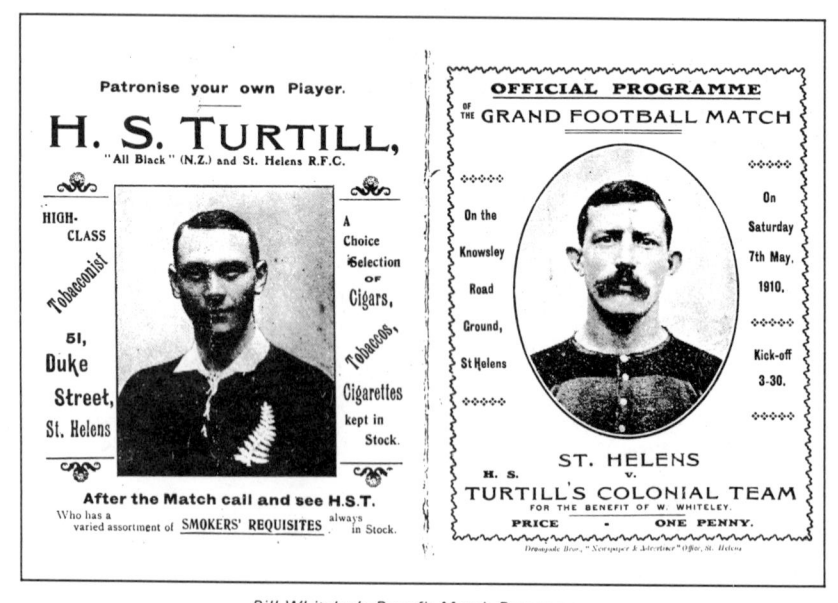

Bill Whiteley's Benefit Match Programme

Barton's Dilemma

In the close season of 1910, Managers Joe Clifford of Huddersfield and Joe Houghton, the former St. Helens Secretary, took the first England touring team to Australia and New Zealand. Tommy Barton's selection was a formality, yet there is no record of his prowess 'Down-Under'.

He did not go because the Rugby League would not make up his wages to his Mother whilst he was away. There were no allowances for single men. His name appeared in the official list, and on several photographs of the party — but he never toured.

High Hopes

There was big news in the Autumn of 1910. Tom Crellin, the big Cumberland forward was coming down for the opening match against the Champions — Oldham. Crellin had signed for the Saints with Archie Waddell, a strapping six foot New Zealander, and another chum of Jum Turtill's. Stan Bevan, the Welshman from Treherbert, completed an impressive trio of reinforcements for the pack.

Enthusiasm was so great that when Turtill exhibited the Saints' new blue and black hooped jersey in his shop window, the Police had to move the crowds on. Season tickets sold like wildfire, prompting this amusing item in the St. Helens Newspaper:—

"The decision of the Saints Committee that season tickets must be paid for when they are bought, is making no difference to the sales".

On the Friday before the Oldham match came more sensational news. Saints had signed yet another New Zealand international — David MacPhail from Wigan. So that ready for the start of the season, St. Helens had a formidable array of talent available:— Turtill, Flanagan, Jimmy Greenwood, MacPhail, Barton, Harold Greenwood, Matt Creevey, Lee, Mavitty, Prescott, Bevan, Waddell and Crellin. Little wonder the Rough'yeds were trounced 16 - 5!

Three weeks later, Tommy Barton terrorized the Welsh at Merthyr with his first hat trick of tries. In those days local tradesmen offered incentives for anyone scoring three tries for the Saints, or three goals for St. Helens Town — who played at Park Road. Stewarts, the tailors in Church Street, offered a made-to-measure suit free of charge for such a feat. As a result of his scoring prowess the previous season, Jimmy Flanagan must have been St. Helens' best dressed man!

In early October, Saints took on the unbeaten Widnes team. Over 5,000 people made the trip from St. Helens to see their favourites go down 28 - 12. At one stage they led 7 - 0 when, for the second time in succession, Barton was badly injured and was laid up for months.

After that, the injury list reached epidemic proportions, with the whole of the three-quarter line crocked and put out of action. Another Colonial was added to the Saints' roster, Upton — the Recs' Australian cricket professional, who had played as a three-quarter, back home in Sydney.

On Boxing Day, Barton, Creevey, Jimmy Greenwood and Turtill — were all on the injured list again, and Wigan won easily 18 - 6 at Knowsley

Road. The following day at Hunslet, St. Helens lost 5 - 3. Jack Manchester, the former Saint who had bought his own transfer in 1909, scored the winning try for the Yorkshiremen — three minutes after time had expired.

As the memorable 1910 drew to a close, the early season hopes of glory had cruelly faded. The poor form continued into the second half of the campaign with Saints finishing a disappointing nineteenth out of twenty-eight clubs. Yet despite the bad results, the first part of 1911 was to contain some unforgettable moments, which Saints' supporters still talk about to this day.

Accidents Will Happen

On a gloomy Saturday afternoon in January, 1911 — the Knowsley Road crowd reserved a special cheer for Saints' opponents, Swinton. They knew that there had nearly been no match at all. The St. Helens Newspaper carried a full report of the drama that had taken place before the kick-off:—

> *"The members and officials of the Swinton team had a rather lively experience on Saturday afternoon while on their way from the London and North Western Station to the Headquarters of the Rugby Football Club — the Talbot Hotel in Duke Street. They were being driven in a three-horse omnibus and at the corner of Lowe Street and Duke Street, where there is a curve, the bus came into a rather violent collision with a tramcar which was coming from Dentons Green.*
>
> *Fortunately, the omnibus was not overturned but the top was knocked off and other damage done while the occupants were knocked about in all directions. Albert Morris, the Swinton wing three-quarter was the most seriously injured. His shoulder and leg being badly scarred and cut, as a result of which he was not able to play in the match and one of the reserve men had to take his place. Others who sustained cuts were Joseph Jones — touch judge of Wigan, Henry Samson — bag-carrier of Nelson Street, Swinton and William Partington, Director of Worsley. William Belshaw of Wigan, a member of the St. Helens team who had travelled with the Swinton players was cut on the leg. The whole of the occupants of the car quickly made their way to the Talbot Hotel and those who were injured were attended to".*

Swinton fought a splendid game, in spite of their difficulties. The finish proved to be a remarkable affair. Four minutes from time, the Saints led by three points — yet a minute later the Lions scored a try and conversion, putting them two points in front.

As time ran out the Saints pack made one last effort to save the match. From a ruck on the visitors' line the ball popped out to a Swinton player, who hesitated for a split second. That was all big Archie Waddell needed to snatch the ball from his grasp and dive over for the winning try.

The Colonial Saints (1907 — 1914)

Poor old Swinton! A road accident and a last minute defeat into the bargain. As they headed back to Manchester they cursed their ill-luck. This was one visit to the pill and glass town they would want to forget!

The Flying Curate

On the St. Helens left-wing in the Swinton match, and scorer of the Saints second try was a recruit of a different character, the Rev. Christopher M. Chavasse. Both he, and his brother Noel, were the sporting sons of the Bishop of Liverpool. The twins made a name for themselves at Oxford University where they won their athletics blues in 1907, as well as representing England in lacrosse. They also had the honour of taking part in the 1908 Olympic games in London, although they did not capture any medals.

Christopher, a former Rugby Union winger with the Liverpool club, was ordained in 1910 and appointed to the St. Helens Parish Church staff. Saints were just the team for him if he wanted to identify himself with his parishioners. When he joined the club, however, he was well aware that by taking part in professional football he could never achieve his ambition of playing Rugby Union for Lancashire.

The Knowsley Road crowd soon found out that the Reverend Gentleman was a real flier on the wing. He scored a marvellous try against Hunslet on his debut, and his speed and finishing ability certainly impressed his team mates. In one amusing incident, Saints' skipper Jum Turtill had reason to rebuke one of his earthier forward brethren for swearing, so as not to put the Parson off his game.

The afternoon of Saturday, 21st January, 1911 was blessed with gorgeous weather. The conditions were ideal for football. A huge crowd of over ten thousand had gathered at Knowsley Road for the visit of high riding Wakefield Trinity. Many people, especially the ladies — had been drawn to the fixture in anticipation of seeing the Rev. Chavasse play.

There was a tremendous cheer as Jum Turtill led his side out of the gate at the railway end. Behind him were familiar faces, Flanagan, Jimmy Greenwood, Mavitty, Archie Waddell, Kelly, Belshaw, Trenwith, Crellin, Prescott, Pope and the evergreen Kitty Briers.

Puzzled spectators counted only twelve St. Helens players. Where was Chavasse? everyone asked. The only explanation they got was that he was held up at Headquarters.

After the game had been started for some time, and Wakefield were eight points to the good, the vacancy was filled by Sam Daniels taking the sixth place in the scrum, with 'Butcher' Prescott going on the wing.

About half-an-hour of the first half had passed when a figure in a blue and black jersey vaulted over the fence and rushed on to the field. It was the missing curate, but his stay was short lived. The referee sent him off as St. Helens already had thirteen men on the pitch. Much to his disgust, he was also reported for ungentlemanly conduct, not having first sought the referee's permission to enter the field of play.

What promised to be a great occasion had fallen flat. Saints never recovered from the eight points deficit and succumbed to the Tykes by 18 - 8.

> "The whole thing was a fearful mull on my part" explained Chavasse later, "and I accept full responsibility for it. I had been up the previous night preparing a sermon, and after lunch I sat in my chair before the fire running through it, when I dozed off. I rushed to Headquarters to find the dressing room doors locked and everyone gone to the match. I obtained the keys and sent for a cab while I dressed, but they had to harness the horse, and when I reached the ground it was only to find that I could not play".

The wisdom of the official in charge of the team was later questioned by the Committee, as he did not bother to send a messenger round to the curate's house — a mere three minutes away. What made matters worse was that the game was patronised by members of the Northern Union Committee — who had come over to be formally introduced to their President, the Earl of Derby.

The affair was soon forgotten however, and the future Bishop of Rochester played at Broughton the following week, helping Saints to win 14 - 7. His Rugby League career was somewhat restricted by his vocation, and he played mostly with the 'A' team, although he did manage to score three tries in six first team appearances. Despite that, the local rugbyites will always remember him most for the game he missed.

Up From 'Down Under' 1911

Saints approached their fifteenth season of Northern Union Football, determined to give their loyal band of supporters plenty to cheer about. the Talbot Hotel remained the focal point of the club, and pre-season training was held there on Tuesday and Thursday evenings at seven o'clock, under the watchful eye of 'Cuddy' Pennington. After a warm-up routine, using skipping ropes in the pub yard, the players would run up to Queen's Park for sprinting and ball practice. They later returned to Headquarters for a work out with the dumb bells or punch ball.

These training methods seemed justified as St. Helens began their league campaign with four straight wins. The biggest test of their mettle came with the visit of the Australian tourists, on Saturday, 14th October, 1911. Kitty Briers told his fellow Saints what to expect. Two weeks before he had made his first county appearance for ten years as the Kangaroos beat Lancashire 25 - 3 at Ewood Park, Blackburn.

The match had certainly captured the public's imagination. As the teams arrived at Knowsley Road aboard the waggonette, they could hear the Salvation Army band entertaining a full house of over 12,000 people. "Fancy playin' on Saints' field and not touchin' the ball" remarked one wag in the crowd.

The St. Helens players set about their task in a way which surprised their illustrious opponents. Jimmy Greenwood gave the homesters a dream start with a well-taken drop goal. A great roar followed as Trenwith picked up from a scrum, dummied one man, and made a superb opening for Flanagan. The winger danced along the touch-line, drew full-back Fraser and gave a superb pass inside to 'Butcher' Prescott, who cantered over amid terrific cheers. Although Jum Turtill failed with the kick at goal, the lead could have been extended further had several chances not gone begging. Saints were to pay for these shortly before half-time when Hallett scored a try. Russell equalized with the conversion.

Despite holding their own after the restart, the Blue and Blacks could not add to their score, and the Australian staying power began to tell. Their late rally realized eleven points, and the game ended in a 16-5 defeat for the gallant Saints.

Everyone agreed that it had been a tussle worth going miles to see. The Australians returned to their Southport base to prepare for their next game. They were to meet England at Craven Cottage, Fulham, the following Wednesday.

AUSTRALIAN TOUR 1911-12
Wednesday, 14th October, 1911
At Knowsley Road
ST. HELENS (5)5   AUSTRALIA (5)16

ST. HELENS: H. Turtill (Capt.), J. Flanagan, J. Greenwood 1G, J. Molyneaux, J. Manchester, F. Trenwith, Scholes, F. Lee, J. Prescott 1T, J. Pope, J. Mavitty, J. Ackerley, W. Briers.

AUSTRALIA: Fraser, Broomham, Hallett 1T, Russell 2T, 2G, Bereery, Farnsworth, McKivatt, Burge, Noble, Gillett, Sullivan, McCue, Craig 1T.

Referee: Mr. Smith (Halifax)
Attendance: 8,000
Receipts: £350

Four of the Best

The St. Helens team continued to thrill the crowds with some superb attacking football and finished a creditable seventh place in the table. Four of the players who starred against the Colonials became key figures in the club's success.

Jum Turtill was an inspiration at full-back. An ever present, his 61 goals in 36 appearances included eight in one match at home to Barrow. The skipper often took to the field sporting a natty pair of mittens in the depths of winter.

In the backs, the combination of Jimmy Greenwood at right centre with the quicksilver Flanagan outside him, proved to be devastating. They shared forty-two tries between them and were feared throughout the Northern Union.

The pack was a solid unit. Experienced campaigners such as Mavitty, Lee and Briers were complimented by the bustling style of 'Butcher' Prescott, whose sixteen tries made him a most valuable asset to any side.

Yet — once again, cup success eluded them. Supporters blamed the Committee for making no attempt to sign a top fly-half after Matt Creevey's departure to Warrington the previous season. It proved to be the one real weakness in an otherwise strong combination.

Kitty's Swansong

After the last match of the 1911-12 season at Hunslet, Billy Briers announced his retirement. He was the last playing member left from the team which had defeated Rochdale in the club's first Northern Union match in 1895. The lad from 'Donkey Common' had played in nearly 90% of Saints' matches between 1895 and 1912. He made a total of 512 appearances for St. Helens, scoring 114 tries. An ever-present in 1896-7 and 1908-09 — he appeared in seventy-eight consecutive matches from November, 1907 to February, 1910. Twice he captained Lancashire, although an International cap eluded him.

Kitty owed his tremendous consistency to a high-level of fitness. He possessed a great turn of speed and had tremendous shoulder muscles for his size. These were developed during his years at Lea Green Colliery, where he was a Blacksmith's striker.

A quiet, steady fellow — Briers never gave up his interest in St. Helens football. Every Saturday he could be seen in his favourite place in the stand, white moustached, gravely smoking his beloved pipe — seldom commenting either favourably or unfavourably on play or players.

He was to die tragically at the age of fifty-six after an operation for Appendicitis in the early 1930's. Tommy Foulkes, greatly upset at the loss of his old comrade, added his own tribute:—

"We played together for many a year, and I never wish to see a finer player or a better comrade. You could always rely on Kitty Briers".

William Briers 'Mr. Reliable'

Season	Club App	Tries	Lancashire App	Tries	Lancs. Trials App	Tries	The Rest (v Champions) App	Tries
1895/6	36	7	4	1				
1896/7	32	8	2		1			
1897/8	20	3	2		1			
1898/9	28	12	3		1			
1899/1900	23	4	3		1		1	
1900/1	29	5	3	1	1			
1901/2	26	7	1		1			
1902/3	34	5						
1903/4	40	11						
1904/5	33	2						
1905/6	29							
1906/7	28	14						
1907/8	33	10						
1908/9	31	8						
1909/10	32	9						
1910/11	23	4						
1911/12	35	5	3					
TOTALS:	512	114	21	2	6		1	

Spreading the Gospel

Kitty Briers was certainly missed the following season as the Blue and Blacks slumped to a disappointing sixteenth place in the table. Rochdale ended hopes of Lancashire cup success, and mighty Huddersfield triumphed at Knowsley Road in the Challenge Cup before going on to win the competition.

Another old favourite, Jum Turtill, had been dropped in mid-November and replaced by an 'A' team half-back! The New Zealander had more luck off the field. Towards the end of 1912 he took over the Nelson Hotel in Bridge Street and proved to be quite a success in the licensed trade.

Everyone agreed that a mid-season break would be just the thing to recharge the batteries. Just such an opportunity arose. Attempts were being made to establish the Northern Union Code in Devon, and St. Helens became the first team to oppose a southern combination in a professional rugby match. They beat Torquay 29 - 5 at Paignton on Saturday, 8th February, 1913 before an enthusiastic crowd. On the Monday it was over to Plymouth, where Saints were again victorious by 27 - 17.

Despite initial interest, no team from the South East ever achieved league status. At least the St. Helens party had enjoyed themselves. Harry Mercer — the Saints' secretary later wrote to the Plymouth club complimenting them on their fine display. Many doubted the wisdom of such 'missionary zeal' as the club accounts revealed a loss of nearly ten pounds from the tour!

Up in Smoke

As supporters still waited in vain for a quality fly-half, the Committee bore the brunt of criticism for the decline in the clubs' playing record. 'Nemo' in the St. Helens Newspaper wrote:—

> "Look at their manner of picking players; centres in the second team picked on the wing of the first team. Halves picked full-back for the first team; centres, half-back — while the regular players of this customary position in the second team are ignored".

How the sparks flew at the club's Annual General Meeting in the Town Hall on 29th May, 1913. The flames of discontent were fanned so much that it was no surprise to find the building gutted by fire ten days later, causing £20,000 worth of damage!

The Clog and Stocking Heroes

The last match of the season at Knowsley Road proved to be a most entertaining affair. Turtill's Toddlers — a team of local celebrities assembled to play a charity match against a similar outfit — Waddell's Warriors, on 17th April, 1913. The game was in aid of the Clog and Stocking Fund, set up by the Chief Constable of the town.

Turtill and Waddell had played for, and captained two similar sides the previous year. For this Clog Fund match though, neither played. The captaincies went to Harry Johnson and Leo Weisker, managers of the Theatre Royal and of the Hippodrome, respectively.

The large crowd cheered enthusiastically as the Rev. C. M. Chavasse, the Warriors' star three-quarter, back again on his hallowed turf, streaked away to score a great try and add the conversion.

Yet the afternoon belonged to the Toddlers, who had a clear advantage because at least two of them understood what the referee meant when he said "free kick". Not that the official, a certain Lance Todd, could blow his whistle all that often — as he was doubled up with laughter most of the time.

Mr. Todd certainly had his hands full. On account of 'disorderly conduct' J. F. May (a future Saints' Chairman) and the Rev. Chavasse were severely lectured for outrageous behaviour, and sent from the field of play.

Hanging chastened heads, the culprits dissolved into the background..... but only until the referee had turned his back. Then it was back to the field of play. Great stuff!

The Colonial Saints (1907 — 1914)

FIRST TEAM GATE RECEIPTS 1912-13

	£ s. d
Barrow	130. 7. 4d
Hunslet	169.17. 9d
Widnes	190.17. 3d
Runcorn	29. 7. 7d
Warrington	37. 3. 7d
Broughton	76.12. 8d
Dewsbury	87.14. 3d
Rochdale	82. 6.10d
Wigan	218.12. 0d
Huddersfield	305. 2. 3d
Wakefield	25.16. 6d
Swinton	77. 3. 6d
Coventry	32. 4. 6d
Oldham	115.16. 9d
Salford	27. 3. 1d
Leigh	40.19. 9d
Huddersfield (NUC)	196. 8. 1d +
Warrington (LC)	77. 5. 5d +

+ Shared gates

Receipts were down by over £500 from the heady days of 1911-12. Huddersfield, with Colonial stars such as Rosenfeld and Gleason, were the biggest draw at Knowsley Road.

St. Helens had a record 1,100 season ticket holders in 1912-13. Cup Ties were all pay.

Local Lads Make Good

The halcyon days of Colonial players in the English game were about to end in 1913. A transfer ban, previously adopted in 1910, was reimposed by the Northern Union Committee:—

> *"No player who has played football in Australia or New Zealand shall be allowed to take part in league football in England unless he as a residential qualification in this country, of two years".*

This duly ended the signing of colonials. No club could afford to bring a new man over and keep him for a couple of years before he took the field for them. The local press welcomed the new policy, and warned of the dangers of relying too much on overseas players:—

> *"The time will come when even the Colonials will not be available, and then what will the clubs who have got their best players by this means, and neglected their home junior talent, do?"*

No-one could accuse the St. Helens Committee of neglecting their local

The Colonial Saints (1907 – 1914)

talent. At the end of each season, the club held a gold medal competition for amateur teams in the town and great players such as Tommy Foulkes and Jimmy Flanagan had joined the Saints after impressive displays in these competitions.

Westfield Amateurs beat St. Helens Rovers in the 1912 final at Knowsley Road. Later that evening in the Talbot Hotel, Saints' officials signed utility-back Teddy McLoughlin from Westfield. Transferred to Rochdale a decade later, he became the first and only St. Helens man to own a Northern Union Challenge cup Winner's medal when the Hornets beat Hull 10 – 9 in 1922.

The St. Helens three-quarters do not give Flanagan enough to do. The speedy wing man has suffered much from "starvation" in the last few matches.

I WANT WORK.

Recs Revival

The St. Helens Recreation team made a welcome return to rugby in 1913-14. Their name first appeared in the Northern Union Cup Competition in 1897, when they were playing at the Queen's Recreation Ground in Boundary Road, yet they were not allowed to join the Lancashire Senior Competition – Salford, Swinton and Morecambe entering the charmed circle of the League at their expense.

The call was then to soccer, and along the Recs went to their new home and code at City Road. Alf Ellaby's Father – Oliver, was one of their stars.

Despite a promising start interest gradually fell away. By 1913 support was so strong within the Recs' sports section for a return to the handling code, that the decision was taken – and the Recs joined the Lancashire Combination. One of their first signings was a half-back turned down by the Saints because he was too small. How wrong they were. Johnny Greenall joined the Recs and later became an international scrum-half!

St. Helens could ill afford to lose such outstanding talent. The great side of 1910-12 was breaking up, and replacements were badly needed in certain key positions. The club did not have the means to join their big-spending counterparts such as Hunslet, who paid £500 for Huddersfield's Edgar Wrigley.

Although Flanagan and Prescott were county players, they were not selected for the trip to Australia at the end of the season. This tour became famous for the 'Rorke's Drift' test, when Britain beat Australia 14 – 6, with only ten men. It was to be the second successful tour for the two managers, Joe Houghton of St. Helens and W. J. Clifford of Huddersfield. Joe had even more reason to celebrate. As a result of an injury crisis, his son made a surprise appearance in an up-country match, and even managed to score a try! How ironic that the first St. Helens man to represent Great Britain should be a comparatively second-rate amateur. Doubtless Messrs Flahagan and Prescott greeted the news with somewhat mixed emotions.

Chapter 5
The Great St. Helens Team (1914 — 1918)

Europe in Turmoil

By the time the tourists returned home in late September, their success had been pushed well and truly into the background. After a series of International squabbles in the summer of 1914, Britain entered the war against Germany. It was to be the most devastating conflict the World had ever seen.

Despite many problems the 1914-15 season opened as usual. The Northern Union decided to allow recruiting on grounds, and to regard the game as a form of wartime entertainment for the forces and workers at home. Mr. Platt, the Secretary of the Union, maintained that serving King and Country was more important than winning medals on the football field.

St. Helens suffered like most clubs, with players and spectators joining the forces, and others taking up vital home front jobs. Several big names were available for selection however, including Matt Creevey, who had rejoined the club at the end of the previous season. Saints' spectators expected great things from the spring-heeled fly-half and his tough little scrum-half partner — Fred Trenwith.

Barton's Bonanza

Yet the biggest source of inspiration came — appropriately enough — from the skipper, Tom Barton. Even at thirty-four years of age he was still a marvellous footballer. He could play with equal power and skill in about any position in the backs. His generalship dominated a game, his tackling and kicking were superb — most of all, he could run. Over 120 yards, Barton was the fastest man for miles around. He won the professional championship at Leigh in 1910 over a hundred yards in 10.1/5 seconds. His feat was all the more remarkable as the race was open to all comers from anywhere in the British Isles.

Barton began the season in fine style, with eleven tries and nine goals from the first six games. He continued to score prodigiously until he was hurt early in the New Year. His vigorous style of play was often conducive to injury, as Tom Reynolds, his close friend — explained:—

> "....He got most breaks — but they were chiefly bones. Ankles, arm, collar bone. Barton broke everything but his neck.. If Barton had Sullivan's genius for avoiding physical trouble, he might have been just as famous as the World's most famous full-back. He could kick further than Sullivan — he was yards faster. At centre or wing he was great. Size, speed, strength and skill — Barton had all the assets, but he also had the fiery temperament that brooks neither defiance nor denial".

The Great St. Helens Team

A relieved St. Helens Committee was able to pencil him in for the first round of the Challenge Cup at Featherstone early in March. Barton proved a match winner once again, with a try in each half. St. Helens faced an even trickier hurdle in round two, against local rivals Swinton. Only two minutes of this dull, scoreless encounter remained — when good fortune smiled on the visitors. Stirrup, the Saints' centre, booted the ball deep into the Lions' half and followed up at top speed. Ryder, the Swinton full-back fumbled slightly and attempted to clear his lines. Stirrup made a frantic charge at the ball which, to everyone's surprise, stuck in his midriff! The young three-quarter from Leigh kept hold of the ball and raced in for the winning try. "A great finish to a rotten game" said the St. Helens Newspaper afterwards.

The 'smash and grab' Saints faced another away tie in the quarter-finals. This time they travelled to Keighley. All over the little Yorkshire town were posters advertising the clash with 'The Great St. Helens Team'. Such publicity paid off with a near four thousand crowd at Lawkholme Lane. Not a point was scored in eighty minutes, and half an hour's extra time was necessary.

Although the Tykes opened their account soon after the restart with a drop goal, the Saints were far from finished. Barton punched a free kick into touch virtually on the Keighley line. From the ensuing scrum the ball came out on the Saints side. Trenwith picked up, yelled the code word "Beechams" and, in a remarkable set piece move — the St. Helens' forwards opened like a fan to allow the little scrum-half to bore through for a sensational try.

The Keighley players did not appreciate the antics of Saints 'Human Torpedo'. They hotly disputed the try, claiming that Trenwith was made to ground the ball twice before he wriggled over. Gill — one of the home forwards, hurled insults at the referee and was sent off. The crowd — not to be outdone, pelted the unfortunate official with stones as he blew the final whistle.

The Northern Union had no option but to close the Keighley ground for the rest of the season. Meanwhile, it was semi-final day at Warrington on 10th April. St. Helens and favourites Rochdale were involved in a titanic struggle which ended in a 5 - 5 draw after extra time. Trenwith was the Saints' saviour once again with his now familiar dive through the opposing pack. Barton's goal-kicking was not up to standard, although he did kick a successful penalty to level the scores.

A White Gloss Finish

St. Helens had upset the rhythm of the Rochdale side by adopting a 'punting and spoiling' game. These same tactics were employed to even greater effect at Wigan in the replay three weeks later. Saints' full-back

Roberts gave them a dream start with a superb drop goal. Rochdale tried desperately to reduce the arrears, but were never allowed to get into their stride — courtesy of some solid tackling by the Saints' pack!

After the breakdown of yet another Hornets' attack, White — the St. Helens' centre picked up the loose ball and hared away down the field. He shrugged off several would-be tacklers, sold an outrageous dummy to the full-back and streaked under the posts. Barton converted with ease and the Saints were well on their way to a 9 - 2 victory. When referee Renton blew the final whistle the cheers from players, Committee and spectators — were deafening. The rugby correspondent of the St. Helens Newspaper was as surprised as anyone by Saints remarkable feat:

> "I wonder what would have been the fate of any prophet who foretold this year's events. If such a prophet had begun by declaring Germany would be fighting England in 1915, he might have been believed. If he had said Germany would be fighting England, France, Russia and a few more — he might have stood a chance of saving his skin, provided he could run. But if he had said the Saints would win every round of the cup up to the final, away from home — he would probably have been extinguished on the spot as a dangerous lunatic at large".

The final was to be held a week later at Oldham on 1st May. Saints' opponents were a Huddersfield side, enjoying phenomenal success. They already held the Yorkshire League and Cup, and had thrashed Leeds 35 - 2 in the Championship final at Wakefield. The rampant claret and golds had similarly disposed of Wigan in their Challenge Cup semi-final, and were determined to make it a four trophy season.

On the Tuesday evening before the final, the St. Helens players held a practice session at Knowsley Road, followed by a hot brine bath at the Talbot Hotel. Everyone was in splendid spirits and quite optimistic about the outcome of the match. Captain Barton, as defiant as ever, declared:—

> "We have drawn with Huddersfield and we may defeat them this time. Anyway we will play them a good game, and I don't think they will pile up the points against us as they have done in the last three matches".

A COMPARISON OF AGE/HEIGHT/WEIGHT OF THE ST. HELENS & HUDDERSFIELD TEAMS

ST. HELENS

Name	Birthplace	Age	Height	Weight	Position
H. Roberts	St. Helens	24	5' 10"	12.08	Full-back
T. Barton	St. Helens	34	5' 10"	13.06	Three-quarter
J. Flanagan	St. Helens	27	5' 8½"	11.05	Three-quarter
T. White	St. Helens	21	5' 7½"	11.06	Three-quarter

The Great St. Helens Team (1914 – 1918)

Name	Birthplace	Age	Height	Weight	Position
H. Greenall	St. Helens	23	5' 7½"	12.03	Three-quarter
F. Trenwith	Askam	27	5' 6"	10.06	Half-back
M. Creevey	St. Helens	27	5' 7"	11.04	Half-back
S. Daniels	St. Helens	26	5' 11"	13.08	Forward
T. Durkin	St. Helens	23	5' 10½"	12.06	Forward
G. Farrimond	St. Helens	21	5' 9½"	13.00	Forward
W. Myers	Leigh	28	5' 10"	13.00	Forward
W. Jackson	Rainford	24	5' 8"	13.04	Forward
T. Shallcross	Earlestown	30	5' 11"	13.06	Forward

HUDDERSFIELD:

Name	Birthplace	Height	Weight	Position
M. Holland	Halifax	5' 6"	12.10	Full-back
A. Rosenfeld	Sydney (Aus)	5' 5½"	11.10	Three-quarter
T. Gleeson	Sydney (Aus)	5' 8½"	12.01	Three-quarter
H. Wagstaff	Holmfirth	5' 9½"	13.00	Three-quarter
S. Moorhouse	Huddersfield	5' 9½"	12.00	Three-quarter
J. Rogers	Tondu	5' 4"	11.00	Half-back
W. Ganley	Leigh	5' 7"	11.10	Half-back
F. Longstaff	Bradford	5' 7"	14.02	Forward
A. Clark	Maryport	5' 10"	13.10	Forward
H. Gronow	Bridgend	6' 0"	13.06	Forward
F. Banks	Purston	5' 9"	13.07	Forward
A. Lee	Ohio (USA)	5' 9"	14.00	Forward
J. Higson	Featherstone	5' 10"	11.06	Forward

The cosmopolitan nature of the Huddersfield team is most apparent!

	Average Height		Average Weight	
	1897	1915	1897	1915
			St.lbs.	St.lbs.
Three-quarters	5' 7"	5' 8½"	11.02	12.03
Half-backs	5' 4"	5' 6½"	10.12	10.12
Forwards	5' 8"	5' 10"	12.06	13.00
Team	5' 7"	5' 9"	11.11	12.06

Above is a comparison of average height and weight – the two St. Helens Cup Final Teams – 1897-1915

No Bonus – No Match!

Barton's boys had fought their way through to their second Northern Union final, round by round – away from home, for ten shillings each per game. Not surprisingly the talk was about money as players stripped in the dressing room at the Watersheddings. They looked forward to receiving a welcome bonus in their pay packets, especially if they were to lift the cup.

The Great St. Helens Team (1914 — 1918)

One of them asked Chairman Tom Phillips what the bonus would be. To their astonishment he told them there was nothing in the kitty, nothing to pay bonuses with — so there was not going to be any bonus whether they won the cup or not! "In that case" — said the player, "there will be no match". He started to get dressed again. The others followed suit until they looked over towards Barton. He was busy lacing his boots as though nothing had happened. A few minutes later he spoke:—

"Never mind that bonus" he told them, *"there's a medal waiting there — win or lose for every man. Each medal is worth at least three pounds, and I am not going back without mine — even if I have to turn out and play Huddersfield myself!"*

The eight thousand crowd cheered as they waited for the teams to come out. They were not to know of the drama in the Saints' dressing room, and that it was all down to the example of one man whether the ball was kicked off in the final of 1915.

"Listen to those people out there" — added Barton, *"some of them must have travelled miles to see the match. We may have had what seems like a raw deal, but we can't let them down. Come on".*

The Captain's words had the desired effect. Saints turned out, but that was about all. The spirit which had carried them through the earlier rounds had all but disappeared. It took under three minutes for Gleeson — the Australian centre, to register Huddersfield's first try. By the time Sam Daniels had scored Saints' only touch-down of the match with eight minutes to go, no fewer than 37 points, nine tries and five goals, had been debited against them! St. Helens were the most decisively beaten team who have ever appeared in a Challenge Cup final before — or since.

Barton — a gallant sportsman to the end, congratulated the victorious skipper Harold Wagstaff, and paid tribute to Huddersfields' 'Team of all the Talents' —

"It is no disgrace to be beaten by the best team in England. We have done no worse than many other sides who possessed stronger playing resources than St. Helens".

No-one deserved a medal more than Tommy Barton. Yet a lesser mortal would not have been playing at all! In 1910 — when his ankle had been wrongly set after a break, he went into hospital to have it broken again and re-set, rather than give up the game he loved. Truly one of the giants of Rugby League, he will always be remembered as the man who saved the Saints' reputation on that rainy day at Oldham in 1915.

CHALLENGE CUP FINAL
Saturday 1st May, 1915
ST. HELENS (0)3   HUDDERSFIELD (21)37
(Record points margin)

The Great St. Helens Team (1914 – 1918)

ST. HELENS: H. Roberts, T. Barton (Capt.), J. Flanagan, T. White, H. Greenall, F. Trenwith, M. Creevey, S. Daniels, T. Durkin, G. Farrimond, W. Myers, W. Jackson, T. Shallcross.

HUDDERS-FIELD: M. Holland, A. Rosenfeld, T. Gleeson, H. Wagstaff (Capt.), S. Moorhouse, J. Rogers, W. Ganley, F. Longstaff, A. Clark, H. Gronow, H. Banks, A. Lee, J. Higson.

Referee: Mr. Robinson (Bradford)
Attendance: 8,000
Receipts: £472

A TIME-TABLE OF DISASTER – HOW THE SCORING WENT IN THE 1915 FINAL:

2½	Minutes	– Gleeson try
22	Minutes	– Wagstaff try, Gronow goal
29	Minutes	– Rosenfeld try, Gronow goal
31	Minutes	– Wagstaff try
35	Minutes	– Gleeson try, Gronow goal
40	Minutes	– Half-time: Huddersfield 5 tries, 3 goals, 21 points: St. Helens 0.
44	Minutes	– Holland try
61	Minutes	– Moorhouse try, Gronow goal
64	Minutes	– Gronow try and goal
72	Minutes	– Rogers try
75	Minutes	– Daniels try
80	Minutes	– Full-time: Huddersfield 9 tries, 5 goals, 37 points: St. Helens 1 try, 3 points.

Do You Come Here Often?

Huddersfields' four-cups season was the last full season of the war. Competitive tournaments were suspended until hostilities ceased. There was no official championship or league table, but newspapers published tables – based on the results of the friendly games. Saints played neighbours Recs for the first time under Northern Union Rules. The difficulties in arranging fixtures were highlighted by the Derby game at Knowsley Road on April 22nd, 1916. It was the seventh meeting of the season for the two clubs!

NORTHERN UNION MERIT TABLE RECORDS

		P	W	D	L	F	A	%
1915-16	Recs	26	15	2	9	255	99	61.53
	Saints	26	10	3	13	188	259	44.23
1916-17	Recs	30	14	1	15	228	211	48.23
	Saints	23	8	0	15	138	266	34.78
1917-18	Recs	29	16	3	10	270	132	60.34
	Saints	18	4	2	12	94	261	27.77

The Great St. Helens Team (1914 – 1918)

They Also Served

Three of Saints' brightest stars — Jimmy Greenwood, Jim Flanagan and Jum Turtill paid the supreme sacrifice while serving their country in the Great War. Sergeant H. S. Turtill became the first publican in the town to answer his country's call in September, 1914 when he joined the St. Helens Engineers. The circumstances under which he was killed are narrated in a letter from Company Quartermaster, Sergeant Harry Mercer of the Royal Engineers, the former Saints' Secretary:—

Dear Mrs. Turtill

I dread the task which I am now performing, knowing as I do the news I am giving you must cause both yourself and the dear little kiddies Sid loved so well, the greatest pain and suffering. Poor old Sid, he has had to pay a great price by sacrificing his life in the cause of humanity, fighting for freedom, and his King and country.

Small recompense though it is, I feel sure it will be some consolation to you to know that his death was painless. Sleeping calmly in his billet — after a most fatiguing day, he was struck on the temple by a piece of one of the hundreds of shells with which the enemy heralded his attempt to drive us back in the morning of 9th April, 1918 — and he died instantly.

To yourself and his dear family — his loss must be terrible to bear, as I know it will also be to the wide circle of friends he enjoyed, both in England and New Zealand. Both myself and his colleagues, tender to you our heartfelt and sincere sympathy. He was loved by all who knew him, and those who — like myself, have been privileged to be his comrades both on the playing fields in England and the battle fields of France, will miss him more than words can express.

I have recovered most of his personal belongings and when things have quietened down a little, I will send them on to you. In the meantime, please accept my deepest sympathy.

Yours in sorrow,
H. Mercer CQMS

Hubert Sydney Turtill 'Prince of Full Backs'

Season	Club App	Tries	Goals	'Colonials' App	Goals
1909/10	35	1	53*		
1910/11	31	1	47	1	5
1911/12	36	2	61		
1912/13	11		19		
1913/14	24		20		
TOTALS:	137	4	200	1	5

* First half century of goals in a season by a St. Helens' player

Jimmy Flanagan 'Wing Wizard'

Season	Club Apps	Tries	Goals	Lancashire Apps	Tries	Lancs. Trials App	Tries	Tour Trial App	Tries
1908/09	28	17	3						
1909/10	35	31		2		1	2		
1910/11	34	30							
1911/12	35	18		1					
1912/13	30	8		1					
1913/14	37	15		2	2			1	
1914/15	32	8							
TOTALS:	231	127	3	6	2	1	2	1	

Chapter 6

Turmoil and Recovery (1919 – 1925)

Back to Normal

The wartime ban was finally removed in September, 1918 and officially organized games commenced in Janurary, 1919 – on a regional basis. The Lancashire and Yorkshire League and Cups would be played, but there was no Challenge cup or championship. Some months later at the AGM of the Northern Rugby League, St. Helens Recreation were admitted to full membership for the 1919-20 season. Thus Saints and Recs took their places in the new league which consisted of twenty-five clubs. It was to be the dawn of an exciting new era of rugby football in St. Helens.

LANCASHIRE LEAGUE POSITIONS – 1919

	P	W	D	L	F	A	Pts	%	Posn/12
Recs	10	3	2	5	68	102	8	40	9
Saints	8	2	0	6	21	107	4	25	11

Players and supporters in both camps looked forward to an exciting full season of competitive football, with the extra incentive of Derby clashes at Christmas and New Year. The Saints were determined to emerge as 'top dogs' in the 'unofficial championship' of the town. On 23rd August, 1919 – the All-Whites opened their account with an impressive 28 - 2 victory against Broughton Rangers at Knowsley Road. Centre Billy Lavin, the latest product from Pocket Nook – scored two fine tries, while the evergreen Tommy Barton kicked five goals.

A week later, it was the Recs' turn to be in the local spotlight. They demonstrated that their claims to first-class status were thoroughly justified by thrashing Bradford Northern by a staggering fifty-four points to nil. Those Saints supporters who made the short journey to City Road could not help but be impressed. The 'Babes' were well and truly launched!

Several of the Recs' team had played rugby whilst in the Army, while others had developed from junior clubs. Saints released some of their younger players to assist them in their early days. Amongst these was Stanley Bevan, who had been signed by St. Helens in 1910, on the strength of his having scored thirty-three tries in one season in Wales. He always looked capable of developing into a front-line performer, but somehow, he never did. No-one could explain why, until it was discovered that the Saints' Committee had brought the wrong Bevan up North in the first place!

The Recs seemed to be settling down nicely to life in the 'Big League'. Unfortunately, the Saints struggled to find their form, especially away from home. When the two adversaries met at City Road on Christmas Day, the

Turmoil and Recovery (1919 – 1925)

'Babes' won handsomely by 21 - 6. Among their try scorers were McComas and Greenall, who might well have been playing for the opposition, but for yet another piece of misjudgement by the Saints' Committee!

Some years before, scrum-half Johnny Greenall, winger Joe McComas, plus forwards Bill Mulvanney and Frank Bowen, had enjoyed some success in the Junior League, and were invited to Knowsley Road for trials. Johnny Greenall was thought to be too small, and was told to come back in a year's time. Although his chums had impressed, they refused to sign on without him. The following week the Recs' Committee snapped up the lot of them. It proved to be a master stroke — one good reason why the Recs were to become such a force to be reckoned with in the game. All four played for Lancashire, Greenall and Bowen even went on to represent Great Britain at test level!

25th Dec	v	Recs	(A)	L	6 - 21
26th Dec	v	Wigan	(H)	W	13 - 5
27th Dec	v	Broughton	(A)	L	0 - 15
1st Jan	v	Recs	(H)	W	9 - 8

SAINTS' BUSY HOLIDAY PROGRAMME – 1919-20

At least the Saints gave their beleaguered supporters something to cheer about with a splendid win at home to Wigan on Boxing Day. Although defeated at Broughton twenty-four hours later, they managed to 'square the series' against the Recs on New Year's Day by nine points to eight. There was further disappointment on the horizon however, this time in the opening round of the Challenge Cup. Once again Saints were victims of their own inconsistency as unfancied Wakefield eventually defeated them after a second replay at Headingley.

Meanwhile, the Recs were blazing their own glory trail in the competition. They beat Hunslet 9 - 0 at Parkside in the first round, Barrow at home in the second round, and staggered everyone by going to the home of mighty Huddersfield in round three and earning a 2 - 2 draw. The replay took place on St. Patrick's Day at City Road in front of 23,397 spectators. Thousands were turned away. Jack Potter, a keen rugby enthusiast remembers the occasion vividly:—

> *"The boards were bulging alright. Many climbed on to the stands to avoid the crush. Some who were locked out actually paid to sit in the upstairs windows of the houses in 'Bug Row' (Windle City) to see what they could of the match. They were up the trees, everywhere!"*

This Huddersfield side was even stronger than the one which had put thirty-seven points on the Saints when the cup was last played for in 1915. Despite the efforts of Joe McComas, who kicked three goals from impossible angles, the Fartowners class told in the end. Ben Gronow scored a try and kicked a goal while Abram registered a further touch-down for the

Yorkshiremen. The 'Babes' were out, but they had made the eventual cup winners fight all the way.

In contrast to their neighbours encouraging first season, it was a case of back to the drawing board at Knowsley Road. Youngsters like Teddy McLoughlin, Charlie Crooks and Peter Molyneux had broken into the first team with some success. There were some fine young prospects 'under wraps' in the 'A' team — yet it seemed as though the Recs had more plums in the post-war pudding, a somewhat ironical situation that would become even more apparent over the next twelve months or so.

Pavilioned in Splendour

The Christmastide of 1920 was one of the most memorable in the history of the St. Helens club. Over 41,000 spectators witnessed the two Derby clashes against Recs and Wigan at Knowsley Road. Although the Saints could not provide their supporters with a victory on either occasion, the club coffers were swelled by record receipts of £2,250 from the two matches. The biggest gate was in the game with Wigan on Boxing Day, when nearly 24,000 spectators watched Lord Derby open the new pavilion on the ground and saw Councillor Evelyn Pilkington unfurl the new flag she had presented to the club.

A description of the new building appeared in the St. Helens Newspaper at the time. To an old stalwart like Bill Whiteley who remembered those cold and muddy days on the waggonette, the premises must have seemed palatial:—

> "In its isolated position the building looks rather small from the outside, but a tour inside reveals it as a splendidly built and most commodious establishment. There is an excellent gymnasium for the players, a beautiful bath — four feet deep and lined with white glazed tiles — 13ft long and 10ft wide, the most capacious bath in the Northern Union. There is a Committee Room, Secretary's Room, shower bath and offices. In short, it is a perfectly fitted and well-equipped football club headquarters, and will be the envy of every visiting club from Lancashire and Yorkshire".

There were nearly 20,000 people lining the rails with long queues building up outside when Lord Derby arrived at Knowsley Road. He was met by Saints' officials and led out on to the field to see the new club flag hoisted and unfurled by Councillor Evelyn Pilkington. After the Ravenhead Band had played the National Anthem, Lord Derby then proceded to the new pavilion, and was received at the entrance by the architect Mr. Wilson, who gave him a silver replica of the dressing room key. His Lordship then performed the opening ceremony and, in a brief speech, said he hoped the premises would long shelter the players of the St. Helens team as well as their opponents.

Turmoil and Recovery (1919 – 1925)

Tom Phillips, the clubs' representative on the Northern Union Committee, thanked him, adding that it was the realization of many months of hard work. Lord Derby then inspected the interior of the dressing room, afterwards being introduced to both teams and a whole host of local dignitaries on the pitch.

Despite the preliminaries, Wigan kicked off on time in front of the biggest ever Knowsley Road crowd. What a start it was! Big Ben Briers caught the ball and fed Charlie Crooks who raced away for the line, kicked over the full-back and only just failed to score. Two minutes later — Teddy McLoughlin delighted the home supporters by kicking a penalty goal to give Saints the lead, but it was practically the only opportunity for cheering they were to have all afternoon. Wigan soon took the initiative. A try by Hurcombe gave them the lead and they never looked back. Roughsedge — the Saints' loose-forward was injured in the first ten minutes, and Hesketh — the Wigan scrum-half had a field day in his side's eventual 22 - 4 victory.

Wigan's costly imported talent had proved more than a match for the St. Helens 'local boys'. The critics urged the club to use the bumper Christmas gate money to strengthen the team, particularly at stand-off half and centre. The St. Helens Newspaper suggested they ought to search far and wide to get the men they wanted:—

> *"Wigan, or rather the sparkling combination of Welshmen representing Wigan, proved beyond a doubt, that the successful hireling finds more favour with the crowd than the unsuccessful locals".*

Yet there were still many outstanding rugby players to be found in the town — but where? Not in a Saints jersey for sure! The answer could be found at City Road on New Year's Day when the Recs, with not one outsider in their ranks, gave a brilliant exhibition of football and swamped their rivals by the record score of thirty-nine points to nil.

The league 'Babes' were far and away the better team in every department, and after the first score — within five minutes of the start, there was never any doubt as to the result. Their pack got possession almost as they pleased and the Saints' backs spent most of the eighty minutes chasing their opponents, who threw the ball about with great abandon.

Pearce — the young Recs stand-off, gave a delightful exhibition, and besides cutting through on numerous occasions — did some fine tackling. Joe McComas managed a fine individual haul of fourteen points and Frank Bowen was the pick of a grand set of forwards, his second try being a brilliant effort.

St. Helens were disorganized by injuries during the match and had only eleven men on the field for most of the second half. Charlie Crooks and the two Molyneuxs were the only players to show anything like their true form.

As they went off to drown their sorrows, many Saints supporters argued that their club had cultivated the rod for its own back. In the days before the Great War, strenuous efforts had been made to develop local talent. First of all the Junior League was formed and put on a sound footing. Then Tom Phillips — the Saints' Chairman and headmaster of Rivington School, began a schoolboy rugby tournament. Thus the schools juniors and seniors were linked up. The feedpipe of talent was completed and the future of the St. Helens Club seemingly assured. But it was not to be. The astute Recs' Committee rubbed their hands with glee at the many errors of judgement made by their Knowsley Road counterparts, and the consequences were painful to digest. How ironic that one of the biggest blows ever inflicted on the Saints should be handed out by St. Helens lads who, by all accounts, were expected to be the club's salvation.

LEAGUE MATCH
Saturday, 1st January, 1921
At City Road, St. Helens
ST. HELENS RECS (14)39   ST. HELENS (0)0

ST. HELENS: Collins, J. Molyneux, T. Gormely, C. Crooks (Capt.), Hanley, E. McLoughlin, Hankinson, P. Molyneux, Heaton, W. Jackson, Bradbury, T. Durkin, G. Farrimond.

ST. HELENS RECS: Bates, Owen, Pyke, Ashall 2T, McComas 2T, 4G, Greenall (Capt.), Pearce 1T, Simm, Dolan 1G, Grundy 1T, Leyland 1T, Mulvanney 1G, Bowen 2T.

Referee: Mr. Jones (Widnes)
Attendance: 13,000

Enter The Little Drummer Boy

The Recs' victory over Saints on Christmas Day, 1920 — began a festive hangover which lingered well into the New Year, and up to the end of March the team had only managed two wins from twelve matches. Although Rochdale added to the gloom with a 10 - 0 victory at Knowsley Road on 5th February, the frail eighteen year old stand-off half making his first appearance for the Saints had certainly caught the eye. He stood well away from the pack, took the ball on the run, put it to the centres and then came round for the re-pass. Here was one outstanding prospect who had apparently not slipped through the net.

Leslie Fairclough had signed for the Saints on Christmas Day, 1917 — when he was on leave from the Army — having enlisted some time previously as a drummer boy in the Fourth South Lancs. Earlier still, he had been a schoolboy star at Rivington Road School and captain of the rugby team from the age of eleven to fourteen years.

Tom Phillips, his old schoolmaster and the Saints' Chairman had signed him on. There was no bargaining for fees but, being specially in favour, he was given half-a-crown (12 pence equivalent today) and told to go and buy himself a packet of fags. Budding stars went cheaply in those days! He returned to his unit and immediately on his release, he was up at the clubhouse to re-sign.

On a wet day in 1919 the young Fairclough played his first match in the 'A' team, alongside a scrum-half called Walter Groves. They beat Warrington, but a little later they went to Rochdale and the score nearly reached fifty against them. It was left to John Foster – the Saints' treasurer, to break the news to poor Fairclough: "Go back to the junior league son, you're too small for us".

Back he went, dutifully, to the local YMCA club. Yet he would not give up easily, and returned the following season determined to make the grade, though it is doubtful at 5' 5" and 11½ stones, whether he had grown all that much more. He spent a successful 'A' team apprenticeship before being given his chance with the seniors.

Fairclough had the toughest of baptisms, playing against that great Rochdale half-back Ernie Jones, who was quite a character. In one game against the Recs – this genial giant put his opposite number Dickie Glover under his arm and ran off with him, much to the crowd's amusement.

Reputations meant nothing to the little drummer boy and, on this occasion, Big Ernie found it extremely difficult to get to grips with his young opponent. It was the start of a glittering rugby career in which he would find fame on two continents over the next decade.

Eventually, he was to re-form the partnership with Walter Groves which, despite a few hiccups – became one of the most reliable club combinations in the league. Although 'Plodder' Groves was an ideal foil for Fairclough, think what might have been. A Johnny Greenall – Les Fairclough half-back line would definitely have been one to savour for Saints' supporters.

Scotch on the Rocks 1921-22

As the 1921-22 season loomed, the Saints' Committee were looking around for a replacement for Tommy Barton, who was now in his early forties and could not be expected to carry on for much longer. By sheer coincidence Wigan were also looking for a last line of defence and turned, once again, to the valleys of Wales. They signed a seventeen year old prodigy from Cardiff called Jim Sullivan who had played for the Barbarians at sixteen.

Trust the Saints to be different. They spent £350 to secure the services of John McCallum, a Scottish reserve International full-back from Hawick.

The new boys made their debuts on the opening day of the season in front of large crowds. At Central Park, Wigan easily disposed of Widnes.

According to the Athletic News, the Riversiders had made a promising investment:—

> "Sullivan, the young Cardiff full-back created a splendid impression by his wonderful coolness, his superb goalkicking and fine judgement. During the afternoon, he kicked five goals out of six attempts, two of the positions being particularly difficult; with more experience of Northern Union rules he will be one of the finest exponents playing the game".

Prophetic words indeed! Sullivan became the finest full-back ever known in the history of the rugby game, professional or amateur.

Tommy Barton 'Captain Courageous'

Season	Apps	Tries	Goals	App	Tries	App	Tries
		Club		England		Tour Trials	
1903/04	3						
1904/05	9	1	1				
1905/06	18	3	2	1			
1906/07	10	1					
1907/08							
1908/09	20	8	4				
1909/10	28	14	7			2	2
1910/11	10	9					
1911/12	13	5	6				
1912/13	22	12	12				
1913/14	20	6	22				
1914/15	30	37	34				
1918/19	2		1				
1919/20	28	1	26				
1920/21	9						
1921/22	2						
TOTALS:	224	97	115	1		2	2

Meanwhile, at Knowsley Road everything was not going quite according to plan as visitors Oldham pulled off a creditable victory. Over ten thousand people saw McCallum embark on his new sporting career — and have an absolute stinker! The Athletic News diplomatically reported that:—

> "He was strange and unmistakably quite out of condition. His kicking was irreproachable but, taken on the whole, he met with rather more than his share of ill-luck".

That was enough for McCallum. The following Wednesday he packed his bags and headed for home, taking his signing-on fee with him!

Next day the Saints' Committee held an emergency meeting in the pavilion to discuss what to do about the man who preferred hop-scotch to Northern Union football. Messrs Phillips and McLean, who looked more like Gordon Highlanders than anyone else, where deputed to follow the errant full-back for the silver! It was a case of 'You'll tak the high road and I'll tak the low road and I'll be in Scotland afore ye'. McCallum had a short start and got to Scotland first, but our two sleuths were soon hot on the trail!

By the Saturday they had tracked their man down to his home in Hawick, and managed to make him understand that they were likely to remain there until he had coughed up. The horrible prospect of unloading two members of the Saints' Committee permanently on his native land clearly un-nerved McCallum, and he handed over a promisory note for £200 — as the banks were closed.

The club had lost £150 in agents fees and McCallum's expenses, and were only too grateful for the increased takings in the Oldham match to cover their loss. Despite the Committee's red faces, the search for talent had to go on. Before the seasons end, they would follow Wigan's example and look towards the tried and tested playing fields of Wales.

Taking the Plunge

The search for Welsh talent began in earnest with this entry in the minutes of the Saints' Committee on 21st February, 1922:

"A resolution was carried that it would be in the best interests of the club, owing to the unsatisfactory displays of the team of late to secure new players — Messrs Phillips and McLean were deputed to visit South Wales to watch some recommended players, and report".

This initial foray came to nought. Perhaps the two Saints officials were still using their Scottish accents. One player under their scrutiny was Johnny Ring who signed for Wigan shortly afterwards and became one of the games' great wingers.

In early March, Tom Parker the Saints scout was sent to Wales to look for a first-class centre. No less than three players from the Pontypool Club caught his eye, and when he interviewed them they all expressed a willingness to come to St. Helens. They were the brothers Stan and George Lewis of Pontypool and Gus Hayes of Cardiff, playing with the Pontypool team. The brothers were scrum and outhalves, and Hayes a centre.

A deputation of Saints Officials including Secretary John Foster, Committeeman Duncan Watson and Parker himself visited the Pontypool ground to see the match against Gloucester. They were equally impressed and decided to try and get the three players signed as quickly as possible. The subsequent wheeling and dealing makes interesting reading from the minutes of the Saints' Committee:—

SUNDAY, 19th MARCH
*A specially called meeting held in the pavilion —
to listen to the report of the deputation*

"The deputation arranged an interview when the Brothers Lewis asked for £1,000 for themselves as a pair. The Secretary made an offer of £750 but this was turned down as being ridiculously small. After some bargaining they agreed to accept £800 cash down, but refused to look at a cheque. As the Secretary and deputation were not empowered to go to this sum, the brothers agreed to wait until Monday for the decision of the Committee; Hayes asked for £300 but finally agreed to £150. Deputation was strongly in favour of accepting the reduced offer of £800 for the Lewis brothers. Mr. Watson confirmed the report.

After discussion, a resolution was passed that negotiations be renewed with the object of securing the three players at these figures. Mr. McLean offered to advance the club £500 at 6% rate of interest — which the Committee accepted. Deputation explained they had left Parker behind to keep in touch with the players whilst awaiting the Committee's decision".

TUESDAY, 21st MARCH
A meeting held in the pavilion

"Secretary reported that he had received a telegram from the brothers Lewis, saying they were sorry they were unable to make the journey on Monday night to St. Helens as promised. Secretary further reported he had sent a telegram asking whether they were prepared to meet a deputation at Pontypool Road and had received a reply that a letter was following; the subject was discussed and a resolution was carried that immediately on receipt of the letter, Secretary was to get into communication with the Chairman and Mr. Gabbott and Phillips — and act as they thought fit with power to go to £1,000 for the pair".

WEDNESDAY, 22nd MARCH
A specially summoned meeting held at the Fleece Hotel

"Secretary read the letter he had received from the brothers Lewis in which they laid down definitely their terms — these were £500 each for signing on, and playing terms to be £3 for a loss, £4 for a draw and £5.10.0d for a win, irrespective of Board money. After deliberate discussion these terms were agreed upon and Mr. Phillips and the Secretary, along with Tom Parker were appointed the club's representatives. Mr. McLean lent the club a further £275 on the same conditions as the £500. It was decided to send a telegram from Liverpool in the morning, informing the brothers that the club's representatives would be coming, and meet them at their home — as arranged in their letter".

The St. Helens officials duly completed the signing of the half-back pair in time for them to make their first team debuts with Gus Hayes against

Featherstone at Knowsley Road on 25th March. Despite being thrown in at the deep end, the newcomers did well. George Lewis got his name on the score sheet with a try and three goals in the Saints' 24 - 13 victory.

The Welsh lads were delighted to hear that they were in the team to play the 'All Blacks' the following Saturday. What they did not know was that they had been drafted into the 'A' team to give them further experience of their new code, and that the opposition came from no further than .....Ince! They soon saw the funny side however, and went on to play a large part in the reserves' crushing 52 - 0 win. It was a much more confident trio who returned to first team duty a week later. Gus Hayes scored a try and George Lewis kicked a goal in the 5 - 5 draw with Warrington.

A Tale of Woe

The Annual General Meeting of the club was held at the Co-operative Hall in Baldwin Street on Wednesday, 24th May, 1922. It was apparent from Secretary John Foster's report that the new faces had arrived too late to alter what had been one of the most disastrous seasons in the club's history. Everything seemed to go wrong from the McCallum fiasco. Poor form and a string of injuries to key players like Crooks and Fairclough were responsible for the team finishing twenty-second in the league with only four clubs below them. Challenge Cup hopes ended at the first hurdle with a defeat by Broughton Rangers. The transfer of two talented local players had not helped matters. Forward Peter Molyneux went to Wigan, and Teddy McLoughlin — the club's 'One little ewe lamb' — signed for Rochdale for £500 and instant cup glory.

Mr. Foster stated that the team's lack of success, together with the expensive Welsh signings had plunged the club into debts totalling £1,452. Despite the outlay, he and the Committee believed they had made a sound investment, and even advocated further signings for the near future.

Nothing Ventured — Nothing Gained

In late July came the news that Saints had signed another Welsh three-quarter. Tom Flynn played on the wing for Talywain, and was recommended by the Lewis brothers who had returned home for the summer. He signed for £350 and according to the Committee's minutes:—

> *"The Secretary was instructed to see the bank manager with regard to an overdraft to that amount and, in the event of a refusal, Messrs. Gabbott and Topping undertook to provide the funds".*

In one of his first games for St. Helens the 'Flying Flynn' scored four tries against Wigan Highfield. Perhaps the shirts of his new team had inspired him. They had been changed to scarlet, no doubt to make the Welsh lads feel at home!

Turmoil and Recovery (1919 – 1925)

An Ode to Tommy Flynn

Now Tommy Flynn, ye've a wonderful way wid ye,
All the scrum halves are just wild for to play wid ye,
And this in passing, the ball goes away wid ye,
Ye've such a way wid ye,
Now Tommy Flynn.

Here's a health to ye,
Now Tommy Flynn
Faster, and faster, and faster agin,
Powerfullest pacer,
Wid steps like a racer,
The other team's lacer
Is our Tommy Flynn.

From a St. Helens Programme of the early 1920s.

The signing of Jack Prosser, a forward, completed the Welsh jig-saw. Providing employment for them however, proved to be quite a headache. In late November, 1922 the players agreed to the Committee's suggestion that "it would be beneficial from a health point of view" — to work each morning on the ground from 9 a.m. until 1 p.m. By January they actually began their new jobs, after several false starts and letters of protest about pay. It was all too much for Prosser, who went back home and thus forfeited his £2.3s.4d. a week as a member of the ground staff.

Saints spectators did not have long to appreciate the collective skills of the Welsh contingent. Gus Hayes was soon on his way to Salford, and Tommy Flynn joined Warrington for £400 in December, 1925. According to George Lewis he felt that his best position was stand-off half, and saw little prospect of holding down a first team place with Leslie Fairclough around.

Stan Lewis's career was cut short by injury. Brother George explained the tragic irony of the situation:—

"We were playing Warrington at Wilderspool. Mick Hanley was outside half for the Wires and came away with the ball. Stan and I both went for him at the same time; I landed across Stan's knee and that was that! He had no option but to give up the game and return to Wales where he worked down the pit".

George Lewis — the last of the originals, remained at the club for over fourteen seasons during which time he became a great captain and leader. He might have been one of the slowest centres in a first team, but he had tactical genius and was among the half dozen leading goal kickers of his day.

In a first-round Challenge Cup Tie, against non-league Wardley at Swinton on 16th February, 1924 — St. Helens rattled up their all time record score of seventy-three points without reply. George was hurt in a tackle early on and had to leave the field for treatment. He returned shortly after to kick no less than thirteen goals from fifteen attempts. It might have been more had he been fully fit. Only Peter Fearis (v Barrow, 14th February, 1959) and Geoff Pimblett (v Bramley, 5th March, 1978) have equalled his marvellous marksmanship in a single game for the Saints.

Frank McCormick says: Save Our Saints

The 1923-24 season brought sharply contrasting fortunes for the two professional teams in St. Helens. The Recs, with Great Britain stars Jimmy Owen and Johnny Greenall, were going great guns and brought the Lancashire Cup back to the town for the first time. They beat Swinton in the final at Wigan by 17 - 0 and looked set for further success.

Over at Knowsley Road it was an anxious and depressing time. The 'speculate to accumulate' policy had backfired with a vengeance. Even before a ball was kicked the club was more than £1,000 in the red. The newly elected Committee prayed for a successful campaign that would help to reduce the financial burden — but luck was to desert them when they needed it most. Results were hit by a crippling injury list, and bad weather spoiled several gates including the 'plum' Christmas fixtures against Recs and Wigan. The financial position worsened and, by the end of May, the original debt had doubled in size.

One member of the Saints' Committee — Councillor Frank McCormick, decided to take matters into his own hands. He realised that the only way the club would be saved was by starting an appeal fund. In January, 1924 he wrote to the St. Helens Newspaper and literally begged the general public and local industry to come to the rescue.

The fund soon gathered momentum; every public house in the town held their own collections. Local businessmen pledged their support and local firms made some significant contributions. In a marvellous gesture, the Recs' Committee

Cartoon of Saints' Committeeman Frank McCormick from the St. Helens Newspaper circa 1924.

donated £20 to their ailing neighbours. Help came from the most unexpected sources. A special matinee was held at the Theatre Royal by Mr. Dunstan's Shakespearean Players, while Dr. Siddall's Glee Club provided much needed funds, as well as light relief in an open air concert on the Knowsley Road ground.

Yet there was still a long way to go. In March, McCormick and Treasurer George Boardman appeared before the Rugby League Council and asked for their help. The Council's reply was as follows:—

> Rugby Football League
> 84 Grange Avenue
> Leeds

20th March, 1924

Dear Mr. McCormick

After hearing yourself and Mr. Boardman on Tuesday, the Council decided to subscribe to your fund the sum of £250 on condition that a further sum of £500 is raised and deposited in a bank in St. Helens by 1st September, 1924. This sum of £500 to be in addition to, and not to include the £270 mentioned by you as having been collected or promised up to the date of your coming here before the Committee on 18th March.

Yours faithfully

(John Wilson)

The popular Councillor was determined to secure the grant and continued his whirlwind campaign in a desperate bid to beat the deadline. He succeeded — but only just! The additional money proved to be a lifesaver, and a relieved McCormick expressed his thanks in a letter to the Press on 29th September, 1924:—

> *".... I think it is my duty, at this stage, to thank all those who have subscribed to the fund and made it possible to start the season with greater hopes than ever. The fund to date stands at £833 gross, and I am anticipating a few more subscriptions to come in...."*

McCormick's optimism was fully justified. The 1924-25 season saw the Saints rise to tenth position in the league. For the first time in a decade they had more wins than losses. More importantly, as a result of the receipts from the holiday matches with Recs (£611) and Wigan (£730) the club was officially deemed to be clear of debt.

Surprisingly, in the light of his success, Frank McCormick resigned from the Committee midway through the 1925-26 season as a result of a 'misunderstanding' — but he returned to the fold the following year. St. Helens supporters, past and present, have reason to be grateful to the jovial Irishman, the 'Moses' who led the Saints out of the wilderness.

Skepper's Supporters' Club

The idea of a Saints' Supporters Club began in the cold damp Autumn of 1923. The wide slopes on the popular side had no shelter for the stalwarts who stood and shivered there. Jesse Skepper, a life-long supporter and 25/- Stand Member, felt that something should be done to put this to right. He wrote to the local papers asking them for the names and addresses of anyone interested in forming a Supporters' Club. "Our object is to shelter spectators in bad weather" he explained — "it would be one of the best things that has happened to the old club".

Eight names was hardly the overwhelming response Skepper had hoped for. Undeterred however, he held the first Committee meeting of six optimistic souls in his parlour in Spray Street. Gradually the idea caught on, and Tom Phillips — the famous 'Footballing Headmaster' became the first Chairman.

The newly formed club held its meetings at the 'White Lion' in Church Street, and several of the games notabilities such as Lance Todd — came down to address the faithful. Subscriptions were 1/- (5p) per member, and the Committee begged and cajoled shillings before the season was out. Whist drives, dances, stop-watch competitions, boxing matches and score tickets were just some of the ventures undertaken by the club to raise money.

The WHITE LION HOTEL

Church St., St. Helens

(Two minutes from L.M.S. Station)

TELEPHONE 602

THE HOUSE OF SPORT

HEADQUARTERS:

St. Helens & District Amateur Bowling Association.

St. Helens Angling Association.

St. Helens Canine Club.

St. Helens R.F.C. Supporters Club.

Referees' Association.

Caterer to St. Helens R.F.C.

WHIST DRIVES and DANCES SPECIALLY CATERED FOR.

Proprietor   -   **GEORGE BROWN**

The first financial statement at the end of the 1924-25 season revealed an income of £598.9s.8d. Frank McCormick's Appeal Fund received £120, a very timely donation indeed.

After much hard work, Jesse Skepper's dream of a popular side stand became reality. One hundred feet of stand was opened for the visit of Swinton on 19th December, 1925. Two years later a further 120 feet of stand was added. The total cost was £1,063 and the structure held nearly 2,000 people.

Other donations were given at various times to the parent club. In one instance £250 was handed over to assist towards the purchase of Frank Tracey from the Recs and George 'Porky' Davies from Liverpool Stanley in 1938-39.

Ever since its inception all those years ago, the Saints Supporters' Club has continued to play a large part in making Knowsley Road into one of the finest stadiums in the Rugby League — a marvellous testimony to the enterprise and dedication of men like Jesse Skepper.

Chapter 7

Rugby Mad in The Roaring Twenties (1926 — 1929)

Back to the Drawing Board

The 8,000 Saints supporters who gathered at Knowsley Road for the opening game of the 1925-26 season against Widnes, were confident that their team's improved form during the previous campaign would continue. Unfortunately, they were in for quite a shock as the Chemics trounced their rivals 23 - 6. One reporter wrote:—

"Not only were St. Helens deficient in hooking ability, but they packed badly, broke up slowly and had very crude ideas of backing up in the loose".

What made matters worse was that the visitors had played for two-thirds of the game with five forwards, Silcock having been sent off. A week later at Naughton Park, Widnes completed the double over St. Helens, this time by the more respectable margin of 11 - 5.

There were far more scrums than in the modern game, and the major task of the forwards was to win the ball for their speedier colleagues in the backs. A solid pack with a good hooker were the essential ingredients of any successful team. Realising this, the Saints' Committee took immediate steps to rebuild the side 'up front'. Brennan — an experienced hooker was signed from Wigan, and Lou Houghton — a local lad with a reputation as a grafter joined Bob Atkin in the front row. Barrow were beaten at Knowsley Road in the third game of the season, but when eight matches had been played, including Leigh in the Lancashire Cup — only two had been won.

More signings were in the pipeline. At the end of September — Ivor Hopkin, a Welsh rugby union forward was recruited for £150. By mid-October, two more Welsh forwards were on their way to St. Helens from Wigan for a combined fee of £200. Percy Coldrick — 36, an Australian tourist in 1914, was signed as cover until the end of the season and Fred Roffey — a second rower who had won every known honour in the game, was in dispute with Wigan and at thirty-two decided it was time to move on. Saints' Chairman — Jim May, saw him as an integral part of his team-building plans and made him the new Captain and pack leader. In his capable hands the forwards became a much more solid unit. Young players such as Albert Heath, benefited enormously from his arrival as did more seasoned campaigners like Ernie Shaw, another Wigan old boy signed in 1922 for £300 — and a typical loose-forward who loved to throw down the opposing scrum-half if he came away with the ball. Even if the referee blew for a faulty 'put in' Ernie would still run around the pack and crash the unfortunate half-back into the mud.

The team soon showed the benefits of greater possession from its remodelled scrummaging machine. Results improved dramatically in the New Year as the three-quarter line — inspired by the genius of stand-off Leslie Fairclough, began to run in the tries. Indeed Fairclough was fast becoming one of the game's great half-backs. A regular choice for England, this cultured footballer rarely tried to make the perfect opening. He would just get his foot past his opponent to make the first centre come inside to take him, then the 'Little Drummer Boy' would let the ball do the work and a try was made.

Captain and goalkicker George Lewis had settled in the left centre position after spells at full-back and scrum-half. His fellow centres included Alf Frodsham — capable of scoring some electrifying tries in his day, and young Billy Mercer — a product of the YMCA Club, while George Cotton and Walter Wright were regular choices on the flanks. Charlie Crooks was rock solid at full-back, linking up with the three-quarters to good effect when his defensive duties allowed.

Backs and forwards combined superbly in the latter half of the season, as the re-vitalized Saints began to climb the table, eventually finishing in tenth place once again. After beating Recs 4 - 2 at home on New Year's Day, they played seventeen league games — winning twelve, drawing one and losing four — scoring 268 points and conceding 128 — a record for half the season bettered by no one else in the league!

Although knocked out by Hull in the second round of the Challenge cup, the Committee were well satisfied with their efforts to reinforce the side. The Saints were becoming a force to be reckoned with, and were ready to mount a serious challenge for honours in 1926-27.

Give it Ellaby — A Crock in a Million

Alderman W. Burrows tells a famous story from the late twenties, of a rugby mad little boy who went to Lowe House Church with his Father. On seeing the figures on the stained glass windows, he asked his Dad who they were. "Those are the Saints lad" — his Father explained. "Which one is Ellaby?" — asked the curious youngster.

Alf Ellaby came into rugby league in remarkable circumstances. Born in St. Helens he had been a soccer player with Rotherham United until knee trouble was thought to have ended his career prematurely at the age of twenty-six. He came home to St. Helens for a second opinion. Ted Forber — the Recs' crack trainer, had a look at him and promptly disagreed with the Rotherham verdicts. "There's nothing here that we cannot cure" said Ted, and he proved himself a good judge indeed.

Shortly after, Ted Smith — the St. Helens sponge man, practically bullied Alf into training with Charlie Crooks and a few more of the Saints lads who trained in the afternoons. No one was more surprised than Ellaby to find himself selected to play in the 'A' team at Broughton. It was a cold, wet day. Right from the kick-off Ellaby caught the ball and just stood and waited, quite lost. He recalled later:—

> "It seemed to me that all the Broughton team got hold of me, and carried me to the biggest pool of water and dropped me in it! They then jumped on top of me. It taught me a great lesson; never again in possession of the ball did I wait a second!"

Despite this early mishap, he seemed to have a natural gift for the game, and made swift progress. Regular training and massage cured his injury problem, and he was soon given his chance in the first team. A slightly nervous Ellaby made his debut against Keighley at Knowsley Road on 27th March, 1926 — and scored two tries. Not a bad start! In his second home game he ran in a magnificent hat trick as Bradford Northern were swept aside — and the tries just kept on coming. He finished the season with nine tries from seven appearances. Saints had found a new star.

Tom Reynolds of the St. Helens Newspaper could hardly believe his eyes:—

> "A miracle has happened. Tom Barton as a young man again, has come back under the name of Ellaby ..... Ellaby is the most astonishing stroke of luck St. Helens have had since they found Tom Barton ..... If Ellaby escapes injury he will electrify the crowds this coming season".

Reynolds was a good judge. In his first full season 1926-27, Ellaby's rise to fame was meteoric. He gained county and international honours, and sensationally established a club record of fifty-five tries for a season for St. Helens. The former centre-half was a 'Crock in a Million' — a great artist and entertainer, and a hat trick specialist, reserving them neither for the good nor the bad.

Ellaby was the great Jim Sullivan's personal nightmare. In an England v Wales match at Wigan, he beat 'Sully' three times for three tries in a feat the Wigan crowd could never forget. Sullivan always was full of admiration for the St. Helens flying machine:—

> "In his prime he could make a full-back look silly with his power of shooting away to leave the full-back grasping thin air. I'll swear too that Ellaby had swivel eyes that could look in two directions at once. The result was that he often had full-backs running the wrong way before they got near enough to lay a hand on him".

A Winger's Paradise

Alf Ellaby's astonishing rise to prominence was a splendid opportunity to play open football, the like of which had not been seen at Knowsley Road for years. George Lewis remembered the instructions they received in the dressing room before a match:—

"We were told to let the ball do the work and get it down the line to the wings as quickly as possible. We needed no second invitation of course, and the wings started running in the tries. Everyone enjoyed their football, why — even Treasurer George Boardman managed a smile!"

St. Helens Newspaper Friday, January 21st, 1927

According to Alf Ellaby, there was much more space for the three-quarters in those days:—

"Unlike today, the play-the-ball was more in the nature of a rugby union style loose scrum. You would have maybe three players on the ground

after the play-the-ball, leaving more room for the backs to show their finishing skills".

Yet it was one of the great spectacles of rugby in the late twenties to see Alf Ellaby in action. Even though he was over six foot in height, he possessed such amazing flexibility that he could stoop when on the run and pick up a ball from the ground with one hand without stopping.

Len Kilshaw — a long time Saints supporter recalled that if George Lewis threw out a high or a wide pass it made no difference, Ellaby would take it in his stride on his way to the line. "He would put the ball down and run away" said Len. "He did not dive to give someone the chance of putting the knees in".

The first match of 1926-27 season got under way with a win at Widnes. Ellaby opened the scoring after a spectacular leap to catch George Lewis's lobbed pass. Although the Chemics gained sweet revenge seven days later, the St. Helens lads recovered with a 15-0 win at Featherstone. The next four matches were won, and Ellaby scorched in for his first hat trick of the new campaign at home to Barrow. George Lewis kicked seven goals, a feat he repeated a fortnight later against Pontypridd.

Non-league Pemberton Rovers had the misfortune to be drawn away to the Saints scoring machine in the first round of the Lancashire Cup. It was no contest. Lewis kicked eight goals, Ellaby notched up another effortless hat trick, and other team members scored at will. According to Bert Wright — Pemberton had been to St. Helens to better their rugby education. In the first of a series of five sketches, the witty cartoonist showed Charlie Crooks with a football, addressing a class of thirteen infants, the lesson being 'How to win t'Lancs coop tha' knows'. The sketches were almost prophetical.

Swinton — the holders, provided a much more formidable obstacle to overcome in the second round. Yet Roffey's boys eclipsed the visitors in a magnificent display of fast open rugby. Fairclough scored one of his 'special' tries, and Lewis kicked seven goals and scored a try in a sensational twenty-nine points to eighteen victory.

Three days later, the jubilant Saints warmed up for their forthcoming semi-final at Widnes by swamping Rochdale Hornets at Knowsley Road. The game was a personal triumph for Ellaby. He amazed the opposition by the ease with which he swerved and side-stepped four or five men while travelling at a tremendous pace to score five great tries.

The semi-final itself was a dour affair, and a George Cotton try earned the Saints a somewhat fortunate draw. In the replay however, Ellaby bagged a brace of tries to send the Chemics tumbling out of the competition in front of an ecstatic crowd.

In the other semi-final, the Recs had beaten Salford in a replay at the Willows, and the two local sides now faced each other in the final at

100   *Rugby Mad in The Roaring Twenties (1926 — 1929)*

Wilderspool on 20th November. St. Helens was a town in the grip of cup fever. Whole families were divided in allegiance between Recs and Saints, and arguments raged fiercely over the respective merits of the two teams.

The Recs — who had dominated local rugby since the war, were in their third final and looking for their second win in the competition. Saints desperately wanted to lift the trophy for the first time and grab some of the headlines away from their City Road neighbours. Only one thing was certain — the cup would end up somewhere in St. Helens.

St. Helens Newspaper Friday, November 13th, 1927

A Trip Over the Wire

There was a mass exodus of over 12,000 'Sintelliners' to Warrington on Cup Final Day. It seemed unfortunate that the two teams could not be allowed to toss for the choice of ground to save their followers a lot of trouble and expense. After all, times were hard, and many regular supporters just had not got the money to make the 'Trip over the wire'.

Despite the difficulties, a crowd of almost 20,000 had packed into Wilderspool on a day spoiled by driving rain. In such conditions, Saints' Chairman — Jim May — had only piece of advice for his team before the kick-off. "Do as the stamp did — stick it to the end".

The rain lashed down as the contest began. At the outset, Tommy Dingsdale — the Recs county full-back, failed to find touch and a scrum was formed on his own '25'. Sparks flew immediately as the front rows greeted each other in customary fashion, and the referee had no option but to warn both sets of forwards. The scrum had hardly been reformed when Mr. Horsfall penalized the Recs pack. George Lewis made no mistake with the resultant goal kick and registered the first points after only a minute's play — a great start.

In the opening minutes the Saints put their opponents under constant pressure. A tremendous handling movement among the St. Helens' forwards saw the leather whipped out to Lou Houghton, who kicked over the defence only for Recs' winger — 'Tot' Wallace to touch down and save a dangerous situation.

The Saints were making an attempt to play the fast open game which had been their recent trademark. A well judged free kick by Dingsdale put the Recs into their first real attacking position of the match so far. The ball was fumbled behind the Saints' pack and scrum-half Greenall got his men moving. A scramble ensued in the Saints '25' and things looked dangerous when Groves was penalized for off-side. Unfortunately, Dingsdale muffed the place kick and lost the chance of levelling the score.

It was a costly miss. After fifteen minutes, Alf Frodsham caught the ball from some loose play and put in a tantalizing grubber kick which caught the Recs defence flat-footed. Les Fairclough — following up, picked up the ball, cleverly on the bounce, beat Albert Fildes with a beautiful swerve and shot under the posts for a superb opportunist try. Lewis converted with ease and the Saints were in the driving seat.

St. Helens continued to enjoy most of the game, and after thirty-one minutes it was time for a piece of Alf Ellaby magic. Receiving the ball from Lewis's well-timed pass, he put in a short kick over the head of his opposite number 'Durdock' Wilson. Full-back Dingsdale was caught out of position, and Ellaby more akin to the code he left behind, dribbled over to score a splendid try in the corner which was unconverted.

As half-time approached, the Recs made a desperate attempt to get back into the game. From a scrummage, Ernie Shaw was penalized for off-side. Jim Pyke took the kick at goal and reduced the lead by two points. Shortly afterwards, Mr. Horsfall blew his whistle and half of Wilderspool cheered with delight.

Back in St. Helens many supporters who had been unable to get to the match had gathered in Hardshaw Street to follow the progress of the game by means of the scoreboard outside the offices of the St. Helens Newspaper. The scores were relayed from Warrington every twenty minutes, and when the 10 – 2 half-time result was given — a huge roar went up from the Saints' supporters in the street. Recs' supporters could be heard saying "Wait 'till the second half — we'll show you!". Saints' supporters predicted another ten points from their favourites. "Ellaby gets two tries every second half" they replied, as Hardshaw Street echoed to the sound of good natured banter.

The teams began the second half in rapidly deteriorating light. This time it was the turn of the Recs' forwards to take the initiative. The Saints seemed quite content to stem their opponents attacks and sit on their lead. In trying to stop a Recs attack, Bill Clarey received a kick on the head and was knocked out for several minutes. After the match, Clarey said it had been a complete accident. "I might have felt it worse if I had got it anywhere else" — he added humorously.

Meanwhile, George Lewis got the Saints out of a tight corner with another fine touch kick. His skill and coolness was most valuable at the time when the Recs threw everything into the assault on the Saints line. Fifteen minutes to go saw no change in the score. The St. Helens tackling was uncompromising and, by this time, the players were hardly distinguishable owing to several coats of mud and the gathering gloom. 'Tot' Wallace could be excused in the circumstances from giving a pass to a Saints' player by mistake!

Six minutes to go and the cup seemed destined for Knowsley Road. Crooks and Dingsdale had a brief kicking duel, after which the Saints' pack dribbled up-field for Wallace to come to the rescue once again. The last few minutes were characterized by a magnificent catch by Greenall in the failing light and an injury to Shaw, who forgot all about the pain when the final whistle blew.

The cheering was deafening. Thousands jumped over the barriers intent on congratulating their mud-spattered heroes. Fairclough and Crooks were hoisted shoulder high and carried through the sea of ecstatic St. Helens spectators to the grandstand where the presentation was to take place.

Mr. Rebbitt — the Lancashire County Secretary handed over the cup to Skipper Fred Roffey amid thunderous applause. This was truly Saints in their glory! After a few seconds, comparative silence was obtained. Roffey said:—

Rugby Mad in The Roaring Twenties (1926 – 1929)

"We are proud to hold the cup. We intended to win it from the beginning. The Recs have put up a good fight, but I think the better team won. Now – three cheers for the Recs......."

Johnny Greenall – the Recs' captain, sportingly acknowledged the Saints' victory. "No use beating about the bush" – said the disappointed scrum-half, "the best team won".

The Saints returned in triumph, first of all to the Town Hall, where a large crowd had assembled outside to greet Roffey and his men. Then it was back to Club Headquarters at the White Lion Hotel in Church Street for a slap-up meal and a celebration drink or two.

At the end of the evening – Ernie Shaw, still recovering from a blow on the head received during the match, was determined to take the cup home to Runcorn with him! After a little gentle persuasion however, Ernie handed it over to Chairman Jim May. That night the glittering piece of silverware found a new home, albeit temporarily, under the Chairman's bed!

LANCASHIRE CUP FINAL
Saturday, 20th November, 1926
At Wilderspool Stadium, Warrington
ST. HELENS (10)10   ST. HELENS RECS (2)2

ST. HELENS: C. Crooks, G. Cotton, A. Frodsham, G. Lewis 2G, A. Ellaby 1T, L. Fairclough 1T, W. Groves, R. Atkin, A. Simm, L. Houghton, W. Clarey, F. Roffey (Capt.), E. Shaw.

ST. HELENS RECS: Dingsdale 1G, Wilson, Bailey, Pyke, Wallace, Greenall (Capt.), Halsall, Higgins, Dolan, Hichcock, Smith, Fildes, Mulvanney.

Referee: Mr. Horsfall (Batley)
Attendance: 19,430
Receipts: £1,192

Day of Reckoning

The first major trophy success for the Saints in the Rugby League proved to be only a minor setback for neighbours Recs as they swept all before them in the League in 1926-27. After the final, the City Roaders embarked upon a tremendous run of twenty matches with only one defeat away to Hull in the Challenge Cup.

By Easter it seemed as though the Recs had gone off the boil. They won only one of their four holiday matches, with Batley ending their unbroken home record on Good Friday. Despite these upsets, they had still secured first place in the League table, and had won the Lancashire League trophy.

Saints form since the final had been patchy and they were desperate to mount a successful challenge for a place in the top four competition at the end of the season. Unlike the Recs, theirs was a happy Easter. They finished the campaign in grand style with maximum points from their last seven games. On Good Friday, the Saints beat Wigan at Central Park for the first time in eighteen years. Over 24,000 spectators gave Alf Ellaby a rousing ovation as he ran in his fiftieth try of the season. Fred Roffey also scored a try against his old club, a feat he remembers with great relish to this day!

Home victories against Swinton and Leigh — together with a magnificent win at Headingley, pushed St. Helens into fourth place. They would have been delighted to just get there under any circumstances, but their joy was trebled because the Recs were their first semi-final opponents in the play-off.

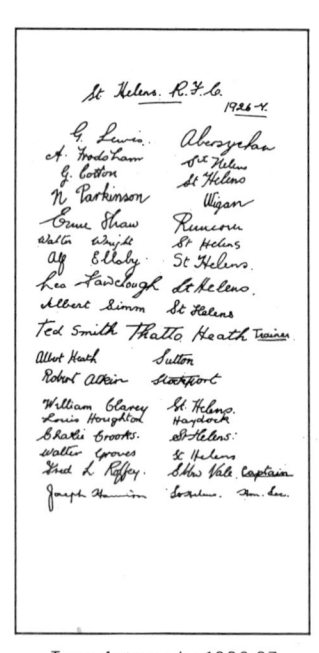

St. Helens Newspaper Friday, January 7th, 1927   Team Autographs 1926-27

On the 'Day of Reckoning' — 19,000 packed into City Road. The Recs lost the toss and faced a strong wind with the sun in their eyes. Instead of playing their usual open game, the Saints made the mistake of kicking far too much. Had they taken a leaf out of the Recs book in keeping the ball down, and not kicking wildly, it would have been to their advantage. The Recreation forwards kept the ball close and were far superior in the scrums and in the open. Albert Fildes and Tommy Smith — in particular were outstanding, but every forward revealed a willingness to back up in the loose.

Rugby Mad in The Roaring Twenties (1926 – 1929)

Johnny Greenall dominated the battle of the half-backs and scored the opening try of the match in brilliant fashion. Shortly before the interval, he fed the eager Smith for try number two.

Recs led 10 - 0 at half-time and the Saints faced an uphill struggle with the elements against them. The atmosphere in the ground was extremely tense and feelings ran high. The game had not been in progress ten minutes before they were fighting like fury behind the goalposts at the top end, and a few minutes later below the stand – and they were spectators not players!

The players, as might be expected – were too impetuous, and the impetuosity of an undisciplined crowd made them worse. Eventually tempers snapped and there was a flurry of fists. The second half had been in progress about eight minutes when Clarey and Smith belted each other in the middle of the pitch. Smith promptly struck Wally Groves several times. Groves retaliated and Houghton and Recs' loose-forward Mulvanney barged into the fray.

The referee – following the play some fifteen yards away saw nothing of it, and a touch judge ran thirty yards on to the field to grab as many of the participants as he could reach. He got Groves, Mulvanney and Houghton – while Smith did a vanishing act. Groves tried to follow suite, but not quickly enough. Referee Chambers came running up and though still ten yards from the touch judge signalled to all three, Groves, Mulvanney and Houghton, to get off.

'Premier' in the St. Helens Newspaper, was most critical of the handling of the incident:–

> *"If the game had been out of hand, if the players had been warned of their conduct and had been threatened with expulsion, one could have understood the outbreak of the referee; but there had been fewer warnings than usual in any game. Without warning there came the drastic expulsion of three players from the game, and subsequent ruin of everything from a sporting point of view".*

Three minutes later Ellaby was carried off the field after receiving a nasty kick on the head. From that moment football was farcical. The Saints had a three man pack, Roffey on the right-wing and Shaw on the left. The Recs went on 'point duty' and the traffic towards the bottom goal was pretty heavy.

Five more tries were scored and matters might have been worse if the Recs had not withdrawn a forward to make an extra three-quarter, and refrained from pushing in the scrums. St. Helens actually got more of the ball from the scrums with their three men than before!

Having gone so far, and having proved beyond doubt that they were a brilliant side – the City Road fiasco was a heart-breaking experience for the Saints. They clearly had an 'off day' and despite the dismissals looked to be heading for defeat. Yet there was never any certainty about a result where a back division containing men of the quality of Frodsham, Ellaby, Lewis and Fairclough were concerned. A defeat of ten points would not have been a disaster but 33 - 0, two men sent off and Ellaby stretchered off was a tragedy from the St. Helens point of view.

Although the Recs lost to Swinton in the final at Wilderspool by 13 - 8, their semi-final triumph was one that the Recs' supporters always had up their sleeves when the Saints' supporters got argumentative. One thing was certain — it had been a great season for rugby league in St. Helens and the future looked bright indeed. Both Recs and Saints had several players capable of being selected for the forthcoming tour of Australia at the end of the 1927-28 season.

LEAGUE CHAMPIONSHIP SEMI-FINAL
Saturday, 23rd April, 1927
At City Road, St. Helens
ST. HELENS RECS (10)33   ST. HELENS (0)0

ST. HELENS: C. Crooks,   A. Ellaby,   G. Lewis,   E. McLoughlin, A. Frodsham, L. Fairclough, W. Groves, R. Atkin, A. Simm, L. Houghton, W. Clarey, F. Roffey (Capt.), E. Shaw.

ST. HELENS RECS: Dingsdale 5G, Wilson 2T, McComas, Innes, Wallace 1T, Greenall (Capt.) 1T, 1G, Honey 1T, Highcock, King, Bowen, Smith 2T, Fildes, Mulvanney.

Referee: The Rev. Frank Chambers
Attendance: 19,000
Receipts: £1,058

Jim May's Touring Seven Stars

James Foster May — Saints' popular Chairman from 1922-31 had, originally, made his mark as one of Rugby League's most outstanding referees. He created a record when he took charge of three Challenge Cup Finals in the space of five seasons just before the First World War. It was Joe Houghton who persuaded the Building Society manager to go on the St. Helens' Committee. In the early 1920's he became Chairman when the club was lowest but one in the League table. Before he laid down the reins of office, the club had won practically every honour in the game. He led the excursion into Wales which secured four players at a cost of £2,000 when — as he put it — "The club hadn't 2,000 postage stamps!"

Iris Hunter — Jim May's daughter, has had a lifetime's involvement with the Saints. Her late husband Harold, was a Director for many years and she has many interesting tales of her Father's days in the Chair. She recalls the time when the old Chairman — Tom Phillips, and Secretary — Percy Else, used to go to Knowsley Road by Horsedrawn cab on match days. The carriage — from Frazer's Cab Company in Shaw Street, picked Jim May up en route at his house in Spray Street. Often Iris would sit on her Father's knee on the journey along the cobbled streets.

> "When Dad signed Gus Hayes and the Lewis brothers, the Committee played hell with him because they had no money. In the end a few of the Committee put their own money in to secure a deal. Father brought the Welsh lads back to our house at 2.30 a.m. in the morning and asked if they could have something to eat. My Mother was not too keen, and so I came down wearing a red dressing gown, and Dad and I cooked ham and eggs for them. Of course, they had had a few drinks to celebrate joining the Saints beforehand, and afterwards they went outside and started singing 'Land of my Fathers' — and woke up the whole neighbourhood!
>
> I remember the time when Dad signed Ernie Shaw from Wigan; he was my favourite. When the club had trouble with money, Big Ernie offered to play for nothing. He was that sort of chap. Dad bought him because Les Fairclough was getting murdered behind the scrum. He had no protection until Ernie came. Father always looked after the players. One day Ernie broke his collar bone; Dad brought him over to the house for a meal and cut his food up for him.
>
> In the kitchen at home we had a large table with green baize cloth stretched over it. A rugby field was marked out on it. All the players used to come to our house — Ernie, Fred Roffey, Alf Ellaby, Charlie Crooks and the rest. They used to work out moves with numbered counters and that's how they became such a great team.
>
> Dad was a fine singer, and many's the time he would give his own particular rendition of 'Ilkley Moor B'aht 'at' after a county match dinner. He was not one for after dinner speeches! Quite often Dad would accompany the players on the piano before a match. Do you know that the Saints are the only winners of the Lancashire Cup to have sung 'Praise God from Whom all Blessings Flow'?"

May was a great administrator, and a member of the Rugby League Appeals Committee. In December, 1927 he was elected as a member of the special Committee to select players for the Australian tour at the end of the season. The genial Saints' Chairman believed that there were a number of players in St. Helens who deserved the chance of finding fame on two continents. Despite the intense rivalry there had been between the two local teams, all this was put on one side when he examined the claims of footballers for the tour. He gave the Recs as fair a deal as he gave to the men of his own team.

No less than seven players from the town were picked to go 'Down Under' for the first time — Alf Ellaby, Les Fairclough, Alf Frodsham and Ben Halfpenny from the Saints, Frank Bowen, Oliver Dolan and Albert Fildes from the Recs. It was nearly four representatives from each team. Only one vote prevented Bill Mulvanney from making the trip with his Recs colleagues.

The St. Helens 'Seven Stars' reflected the strengths of their respective clubs. Ellaby, Frodsham and Fairclough were among the most dangerous backs in the game. Ben Halfpenny — a snip at £250 from Widnes at the start of the season was a running forward ahead of his time. Weighing over thirteen stone, he could do 100 yards in under eleven seconds. All the Recs selections were from their formidable pack. Runcorn born Albert Fildes was a big brainy footballer and a deadly tackler. Oliver Dolan was a reliable hooker and Frank Bowen another big bustling forward.

The decision to include the St. Helens stars caused some controversy in rugby league circles, and Jimmy May was told in no uncertain terms that his 'Swans were Geese'. Alf Ellaby remembers that when they left Tilbury on 25th April, they were not given too much hope of retaining the Ashes. The Australians tended to agree, especially when the tourists won only two of their opening six matches.

Yet as the tour went on, team work and confidence improved enormously. Both series against Australia and New Zealand were won by two tests to one. The Tourists won the first two tests against the Kangaroos, at Brisbane and Sydney — with Alf Ellaby scoring vital tries in both of them. The 'Tin Hare' as the Aussies called him, scored no less than twenty tries on the tour, including four in five test matches. The pack was the mainstay of the side however, and only eight forwards were used in the six tests.

The 1928 Rugby League Lions had made the critics eat their words, and they returned home in triumph, via Fiji, Hawaii and Canada. Financially the tour had been a roaring success, earning the players a well-deserved bonus of £136 per man. The jubilant party landed at Liverpool on 28th September — suitably refreshed for their own domestic season which had just begun.

Later the following month, all the 'Seven Stars' paid their own special tribute to J. F. May as Les Fairclough presented him with a magnificent silver trophy with the inscription 'Presented to J. F. May by the St. Helens' Tourists of the 1928 Australian Team'.

No one had deserved it more. As one of the speakers remarked during the ceremony, the players of the rugby league all realised they had in Mr. May — an approachable friend, no matter what team they happened to belong to.

1928 'Seven Stars' to Australia

	Apps	Tries	Goals	Pts
F. Bowen	16	2	0	6
O. Dolan	7	0	1	2
A. Ellaby	14	20	2	64
L. Fairclough	12	11		33
A. Fildes	13	3	0	9
A. Frodsham	17	15	0	45
B. Halfpenny	10	8	0	24

Test Matches

	Apps	Tries
A. Ellaby	5	4
L. Fairclough	4	5
A. Fildes	6	0
A. Frodsham	2	0
F. Bowen	3	1

Chapter 8
The Team of All The Talents
(1930 – 1932)

PART ONE – THE SEEDS OF GLORY

Enterprise Unlimited

The Hull club created quite a sensation in June, 1981 when they signed three New Zealand test stars, Kemble, O'Hara and Leuluai – who had just completed a successful tour of England. It was a case of deja vu for many older Saints' supporters however, who were able to recall a similar occurrence some fifty years previously. Three top class Kiwis – winger Roy Hardgrave and forwards Lou Hutt and Trevor Hall, joined St. Helens for the start of the 1929-1930 season, making the Saints one of the strongest outfits in the league.

All three had played in the final test at Christchurch against the 1928 Tourists, which Great Britain won 6 – 5. Some months later Roy Hardgrave wrote to his former adversary Alf Ellaby – expressing a desire to play in England. Ellaby immediately contacted the Committee with regard to bringing him to St. Helens. Shortly afterwards at an emergency Committee meeting, it was resolved to sign Hardgrave – and a cable was despatched to Mr. Griffiths, the man 'Down Under' acting on the player's behalf.

Four days later, another special Committee meeting was held to settle Hardgrave's travel arrangements to Britain. Chairman Jim May revealed further details from Mr. Griffiths, concerning two other New Zealand internationals – forwards Hutt and Hall who wanted to play for the Saints. Their stated playing terms were most favourable, and the Committee did not need a second invitation to sign them up at the same time.

Secretary – Joe Harrison arranged for passage to be paid for the three players and their wives aboard the S.S. Corinthic – departing on 3rd July for Southampton. Hardgrave's signing on fee was £100, Hutt and Hall asked for £50. Half was to be paid to them before embarkation, on condition they agreed to sign for St. Helens immediately they arrived in England some six weeks later.

A deputation of four travel-weary Saints' Committeemen – Jim May, Bill Simister, Frank Jones and Harry Ince, arrived in Southampton in the early hours of Tuesday 13th August after an exhausting journey from Liverpool. Les Fairclough accompanied them to greet his old acquaintants from the 1928 tour.

The party rose bright and early at six o'clock and headed towards the dockside, only to find that the Corinthic's arrival had been delayed because

The Team of All The Talents (1930 – 1932)

of fog in the Channel. Bill Simister cursed his luck. Not only had he got to bed at an unearthly hour, but he had been allocated a room in the corner of the hotel where the milk traffic passed, and he did not get a wink of sleep for the rattle of milk cans. His fellow Committeemen seemingly had little sympathy for him and pondered over the possibility of a trip to Cowes!

There was plenty of time to kill. They even sang a medley of hymns which greatly intrigued a party of Americans who were boarding a large ocean-going liner nearby. The Yanks applauded vigorously, no doubt demonstrating how debased their ear for music must have been! The party then came across two men fishing on the quayside. Frank Jones asked if they had caught anything, and one of the men pulled up a keep-net full of little black and white fishes. This sight triggered off Tom Reynolds' imagination. Tom had joined the party on behalf of the press. They reminded him of the Saints' Annual General Meeting. He later wrote:

> "Their little mouths kept opening and shutting — said nowt worth mentioning, and the sides of their little heads corresponding to their ear-pieces were going up and down, along with their eye-brows. It was like meeting old friends".

Finally, at about 11 o'clock the Corinthic slowly drew up alongside the quay, and Leslie Fairclough shouted a Maori greeting 'Kia Ora, Kia Ora" at the top of his voice. 'Kia Ora, Kia Ora" came back immediately from the ship. Two big men and one smaller one, with several ladies, recognized Leslie instantly and were waving to him from the second deck amidships. When in Southampton of course, do as the New Zealanders do, and the Saints deputation promptly Kia Ora'd in Unison — causing a man watching close by to remark "bloomin' foreigners comin' 'ere, takin' the bread and butter", etc. In his case, it looked to be more likely beer than bread!

Within an hour of landing, the three New Zealanders were signing on the dotted line for the Saints in the South Eastern Hotel. The deputation, including the luckless Bill Simister, could rest easy in their beds that night, happy in the knowledge of a job well done.

Lou Hutt told the deputation:—

> "We are anxious to justify the confidence you place in us, and as soon as we can get settled down all round with the strangeness worn off, we believe we shall succeed in doing so".

The St. Helens Newspaper praised the Committee and suggested that 'Enterprise Unlimited' should be their telegraphic address from now on. Striking tributes to the importance of the New Zealand signings were given from the sports pages of some newspapers just received from 'Down Under'. According to the Auckland Star — Hutt and Hall, both forwards with the Ponsonby Club, were two of the finest in the game. Hutt in particular was 'The Daddy of them all' — a superbly built man difficult to tackle, who had the pace to play in the three-quarters in an emergency. Hardgrave, the

'Newton Flyer' was at 10st. 12 lbs. and 5' 7" an elusive runner, with a skipping sidestep that baffled opposing full-backs.

On the Saturday after their arrival, the Kiwis were left in no doubt as to what their signing had meant to the St. Helens faithful. At the end of the club's practice match at Knowsley Road, spectators from all sides rushed across the field to the front of the main stand just like the rush to watch the presentation of a cup, or medals after a cup final. There they stood — just to stare at their new heroes, who had been sitting in the front row of the stand watching the match.

'Great Expectations'

On 31st August, 1929 — there were well over 10,000 spectators at Knowsley Road to see the New Zealanders make their debuts in the traditional opening game against Widnes. Unfortunately, the Chemics pulled of a shock Derby win by one try to nil. The St. Helens all-star line-up rarely extended the visitors, who had a real match winner in their South African second row forward George Van Rooyen. Little did George Lewis's lads realise it, but the former Hull K.R. giant was going to be an even bigger thorn in their flesh before the end of the campaign.

While the Saints had all the makings of a superb team, they were no more immune from disappointment than anyone else. Salford won 13 - 3 at the Willows to send them tumbling out of the Lancashire Cup in a second-round replay. In the face of adversity, however, St. Helens followers never lost their sense of humour. At Salford a Saints supporter was shouting for all he was worth for Roy Hardgrave, who was having a torrid time against his opposite number. A Salford spectator, obviously of Jewish extraction asked him where Hardgrave came from. "New Zealand", the Sintelliner replied. "And do you bring players from New Zealand to try and beat Salford?" he enquired. "Aye lad", the Saints supporter retorted — "but we don't bring supporters from Jerusalem!"

By mid-November the team began to show the consistency everyone had hoped for by winning six matches on the trot. On the sixteenth of that month, the Saints drew 18 - 18 with the mighty Australian Tourists. For the likes of Ellaby, Fairclough, Halfpenny and the New Zealanders, it was a case of renewing old friendships. Ellaby missed the match through injury, and Ben Halfpenny — who had something to prove after his disappointing tour of 1928 — was taken out of the pack to replace him. The 'Widnes Flyer' thrilled the 9,500 crowd with two well-taken tries. On the other flank, little Hardgrave also bagged a brace of tries against his international rivals.

AUSTRALIAN TOUR 1929-30
Saturday, 16th November, 1929
At Knowsley Road
ST. HELENS (5)18   AUSTRALIA (18)18

The Team of All The Talents (1930 — 1932) 113

ST. HELENS: C. Crooks, R. Hardgrave 2T, G. Lewis (Capt.) 3G, W. Mercer, B. Halfpenny 2T, L. Fairclough, W. Groves, L. Hutt, R. Unwin, L. Houghton, J. Arkwright, E. Hill, T. Hall.

AUSTRALIA: Laws 1G, Finch 2T, 2G, Maher, Gorman, Upton, Hadwell, Holmes 1T, Brogan, Justice, Root, O'Dempsey, Armbruster, Kingston 1T.
Referee: Mr. Horsfall (Batley)
Attendance: 10,000
Receipts: £903

BERT WRIGHT'S CARICATURES AT THE ST. HELENS–AUSTRALIAN MATCH, WHICH WAS DRAWN, each side scoring eighteen points.

Liverpool Evening Express, November 18th, 1929

The Team of All The Talents (1930 – 1932)

Despite being elated with their team's inspired form, the Committee had problems. They were finding difficulty in obtaining suitable work for the New Zealanders, a situation that would come to a head in the not too distant future. On the financial front, although gates had improved, wages had increased and money was tight. An offer of £450 was accepted from the Recs for transfer listed Alf Frodsham to ease the financial burden. Secretary Joe Harrison was also instructed to send out a final note to all season ticket holders who still had not paid up!

These same supporters felt even less like paying up on New Year's Day when a Bill Mulvanney try secured victory for the Recs in a dour struggle at Knowsley Road. Something of a minor slump followed, with heavy defeats at Oldham and Warrington. It didn't last for long! Rochdale were thrashed 32 – 5 putting the players in good heart for the first round of the Challenge Cup, and what a match it promised to be. Fate decreed that Saints would meet the old enemy – Recs, at Knowsley Road!

Arguments raged in the pubs in St. Helens, just as they had done in 1927 over the merits of the two sides. Yet the fiercest argument of all came in the Saints' Boardroom, on the day they were supposed to be picking the team! Strong words passed between Harry Ince and Joe Harrison over a trivial matter which turned into a full-blown scuffle. Thankfully, the Chairman's glasses were the only casualty, though for a few moments the two Committeemen slugged each other around with a Christian fervour which befitted a Board that sang hymns every time they won a match!

The Order of the Boot

A few days later over 17,000 packed into Knowsley Road to witness a fight of more epic proportions along typical cup tie lines. The undoubted highlight of an even first half was the kicking 'duel' between Dingsdale – the Recs' 'Shooting Star' and a comparatively untried performer Jack Arkwright.

In the muddy conditions, the normally reliable George Lewis failed with several attempts at goal early on. After thirteen minutes, St. Helens were awarded another kickable penalty, albeit from an awkward angle. Lewis handed the ball to Arkwright who fancied his chances even though he had never kicked before in a competitive match! The big prop gave the leather an almighty thump and watched it sail between the posts to equalize Dingsdale's earlier goal for the Recs.

The former Sutton Commercial forward kicked another two penalties to Dingsdale's one to give Saints a 6 – 4 lead, but just before half-time – disaster struck. Somewhat against the run of play, Albert Fildes worked a try along the blind side of the scrum to regain the lead for the visitors.

In the second half however, the Recs' pack which used to be the great strength of the team, was beginning to buckle under the increasing weight of the St. Helens attacks. The younger Saints forwards such as Halfpenny, Hall and Harrison – were more suited to the furious pace of the match than their counterparts, and gradually gained the upper hand. It came as no surprise when Alf Ellaby scampered over to register the Saints' winning try after a typically crisp passing movement from the backs. 'Arkie' hit the upright with the conversion, but his 'emergency' place kicking had been an inspiration to his team mates at such a critical stage of the game.

St. Helens Newspaper Friday, February 14th, 1930

Two Lovely Black Eyes

Over 4,000 cup crazy Saints' supporters travelled to Headingley for the Roses clash with Leeds in round two. The huge crowd looked forward to a feast of open rugby from two sides on the top of their form. Although the

Saints showed flashes of superb team work to win by 18 – 5, the match proved to be a niggling ill-tempered affair. Play was punctuated by some disgraceful brawling which led to three players being sent off and an emergency meeting of the Rugby League Council some forty-eight hours later.

Moores – the Leeds centre, received a four match suspension for a late tackle on Ellaby. His team mate Pascoe, received a three match ban together with Halfpenny of the Saints. League Secretary – John Wilson, wrote to the two clubs expressing the hope that they would do their utmost to prevent any recurrence of such behaviour in the future.

'Ave We Dropped our Aitches?

The Saints licked their wounds and produced a devastating display of attacking rugby to dispose of Hunslet at Knowsley Road in the third round. Alf Ellaby, the 'Hat Trick King' – thrilled the 19,000 crowd with another effortless three try burst. The twin towers of Wembley were beckoning, yet there was one last hurdle to overcome. The draw paired St. Helens with cup holders Wigan who had beaten Dewsbury 13 - 2 in the first cup final held at the Empire Stadium, twelve months earlier.

When the Saints' Committee met on the Sunday before the big match to pick the team, they again got something they had not bargained for. Secretary – Joe Harrison, read out a letter from the New Zealand players who were refusing to play in the semi-final until certain demands were met by the Committee.

Hutt, Hall and Hardgrave's letter to the Committee

Dear Sirs,

The undermentioned are desirous of conveying the following petition and hope that the same meets with your approval. Should this petition be refused we, the undersigned, declare that we will not continue playing.

Firstly, in reference to working wages, we desire a guarantee of £3.10s.0d. a week for the fifty-two weeks of the year, regardless of football earnings. The work found for us was found to be absolutely unsatisfactory – both from the wage point of view and as a footballer's occupation.

Secondly, we want a written guarantee of £250 each as a retaining fee. We know, as everyone knows, that there has never been a Saints team like the present one, and we think we are worthy of consideration. We came for practically nothing, and now that we have proved ourselves, we feel quite justified in placing these claims before you. Hoping this meets with your approval.

L. Hutt, T. Hall, R. Hardgrave

The three New Zealanders were invited before the Committee and

Saints V. Wigan, Boxing Day 1920.
The imposing figure of Lord Derby at Knowsley Road prior to the opening of the new pavilion. Charlie Crooks pictured right, and his team-mates wore Lord Derby's racing colours of white shirts and black shorts for this particular match.
(Photo courtesy St. Helens Library)

The scarlet-shirted Saints line up at City Road in the early 1920's displaying nearly £2,000 of Welsh talent. Gus Hayes (with ball) captains the side. Tommy Flynn is next to him on the right. George Lewis is kneeling down on the left of the front row, brother Stan on the right.

(Photo courtesy L. Kilshaw)

Jesse Skepper,
Founder of the Saints' Supporters Club in 1924.
(Photo courtesy Mrs. Elliot)

The "Old Enemy" Parade the Silverware

Back row l to r:— T. Smith, W. Mulvanney, A. Fildes, Ramsdale, J. Hughes, H. Grundy.
Front row l to r:— J. McComas, J. Pyke, J. Greenall (Capt.), Col. Norman Pilkington, J. Owen, F. Halton, T. Gormley, T. Dingsdale.

(Photo courtesy W. Greenall)

Jesse Skepper's lapel badge.
(Courtesy Mrs. Elliot)

On The Threshold of Glory

Back row l to r (Players only):— W. Clarey, Foster, P. Molyneux, E. Shaw, B. Briers, Fisher.
Middle row l to r:— A. Frodsham, W. Wright, C. Crooks, T. Flynn, G. Cotton, Woodward.
Front row l to r:— L. Fairclough (Capt.), G. Lewis, Lightfoot.

White jerseys with red crest and arm bands had been the first choice colours since the previous season, 1924/25.

(Photo courtesy Mrs. Skepper)

*Fred Roffey,
Saints' pack leader and
Captain in 1926/27,
wearing his Welsh
International jersey and cap.*

(Photo courtesy F. Roffey)

*Fred Roffey,
the "Senior Pro"
outside his Kendal home,
Summer 1984 —
a member of the Saints'
Past Players' Association
at 90 years of age!*

St. Helens Chairman Jim May presents Skipper Fred Roffey with his Welsh cap before the home game with Widnes on 4th September, 1926. The recently completed Supporters Club Stand is in the background.
(Photo courtesy F. Roffey)

Lancashire Cup Winners 1926/27
The team that brought the first major honour to Knowsley Road.
Back row l to r:— Ted Smith (Trainer), Mr. Horsfall (Referee), Lou Houghton, Ernie Shaw, Fred Roffey (Capt.), Bob Atkin, Bill Clarey, Fred Herbert (Groundsman) Cuddy Pennington (Ass. Trainer).
Middle row l to r:— Alf Ellaby, George Lewis, Charlie Crooks, Alf Frodsham, George Cotton, Albert Simm.
Front row l to r:— Les Fairclough, B. Wilson (Mascot), Walter Groves.
(Photo courtesy Mrs. Cotton)

The 'Hat-Trick King'
Alf Ellaby pictured on a cigarette card of the late 1920's.
(Courtesy C. Johnstone)

A Token of Esteem
Leslie Fairclough presents the Tourists' Australian Cup to Saints popular Chairman, Jim May.
(Photo courtesy Mrs. Hunter)

A Deadly Duo
Walter Groves and Leslie Fairclough, a great half-back combination.
(Photo courtesy Mrs. Skepper)

Jim May (centre with Fedora) at a county match in the early 1930's.
Bob Anderton, the Warrington Secretary is next to him on the right, smiling broadly.
(Photo courtesy Mrs. Hunter)

In the days when rival full-backs often fought long kicking duels, Charlie Crooks, seen here in his Lancashire jersey, was a rock-solid custodian for the Saints.

Saints' Australian Tourists 1928
*Left to Right — Alf Ellaby, Les Fairclough, Alf Frodsham and Ben Halfpenny.
(Photo courtesy Mrs. Skepper)*

Lou Hutt, Saints' dynamic Kiwi Forward.
(Photo courtesy Mrs. Skepper)

Wembley 1930
Widnes Captain Paddy Douglas tries to break through the Saints' cover defence of Billy Mercer (left) and Alf Ellaby.
(Photo courtesy M. Flynn)

Saints at the Double!

League Champions and Lancashire League Winners 1932.

Back row l to r:— F. Jones (Chairman), S. Morris (V. Chairman), T. Winnard, J. Garvey, J. Arkright, B. Halfpenny, E. Hill, R. Atkin, J. Houghton (Treasurer).

Front row l to r:— R. E. Jones, H. Frodsham, W. Groves, G. Lewis (Capt.), W. Mercer, R. Hardgrave, J. Marsh.

(Photo courtesy St. Helens R.L.F.C.)

He Shall Not Pass

*'Big Arkie' Down-Under with Great Britain in 1936.
The look on the Australian full-back's face tells it's own story!*

(Photo courtesy J. Arkwright)

Diamond Jubilee Season 1935/36 v Oldham at Watersheddings.

Back row l to r:— C. Pennington (Ass. Trainer), G. Lewis, T. Hall, A. Lemon, R. Atkin, D. Cotton, J. Bradbury, A. Owen (Committee), J. Carson (Trainer).

Front row l to r:— T. Holsgrove, A. Butler, W. Mercer (Capt.), I. Davies, O. Griffiths, P. Smith.

Seated on grass — C. Glover, H. Frodsham.

Bradbury's 'Boys' — A Saints line-up in 1936/37

Back row l to r:— J. King, A. Cross, E. Hughes, W. Hough, P. Dullard, L. Garner, I. Davies, Trainer.
Front row l to r:— O. Jones, T. Parkinson, J. Bradbury (Capt.), A. Butler, J. Hesketh, Stevens.

(Photo courtesy A. Cross)

Going Public

Saints' first game as a Limited Liability Company, against Widnes at Knowsley Road in 1937/38. Bradbury is the Saints player being tackled, with Ted Beesley behind him. Note the unusual St. Helens jerseys and the old scoreboard in the background.

(Photo courtesy E. Beesley)

The Team of All The Talents (1930 – 1932)

Chairman Jim May asked them to leave the matter over until the Monday night after the semi-final. Lou Hutt, speaking on the players' behalf, refused point blank – as previous attempts to obtain the Committee's consideration by polite means had been brushed aside. The Committee decided not to agree to their demands and would pick the team without them. As Hutt departed, he remarked that there was nothing left to do but look up the times of the sailings back to New Zealand.

"It's like having a pistol at our backs" – said Jim May after the meeting, *"and we will not be treated in that fashion. These lads have been well paid and were given the signing-on fees they asked for. Work had been found for them and their wages had been supplemented by the club".*

The Committee had got a tremendous bargain with the New Zealand players. Most Saints' supporters however, believed that the Kiwis had signed on for £300 each. They were quite surprised at the actual figure of £50 – especially when it was revealed that this included passage money for them and their wives as well. Lou Hutt said:–

"A good forward in England today cannot be bought for under £500". We accepted the club's original terms and committed ourselves to the Saints. All we want is for the club to redeem the promise they gave us about finding us jobs as motor drivers and not a labourer's job. No professional footballer can work like a bullock all week and tear up and down for eighty minutes on a Saturday afternoon".

Trevor Hall pointed out that unless they agreed they would be dependent upon their playing wages only. "we cannot live on playing money when there are no matches from April to September" – he maintained. The Kiwis wanted the jobs they were promised at the start, or £3.10s.0d. per week. "We do not want the £3.10s.0d. for doing nothing" added Hutt, "we merely want the club to keep its promise".

The £250 mentioned in their letter was intended to take the place of a proper signing-on fee or, alternatively, a proper guaranteed benefit. The Committee had to explain that they could not bind a future Committee to that agreement, but they would recommend the granting of a benefit after seven years notice. Such a conditional guarantee from a Committee who had already failed to keep their promise with the provision of work, did not impress the three men much. "It looks as though it's the Corinthic for us in April if we cannot settle this week" – said Roy Hardgrave with a shrug of resignation.

On the Tuesday before the match the situation still remained in deadlock. It was going to need someone with a Kissinger-like flair for diplomacy to bring the two sides together. Alderman Tom Boscow was just such a man. The Mayor was a red-hot Saints supporter, and took it on himself to arbitrate in the dispute. He invited the New Zealanders to tea in the Mayor's Parlour with several members of the Committee. The prospects of beating

Wigan increased dramatically during the next few hours! It was agreed that if the Committee would discuss the situation in full after the Cup-tie, the Kiwis would withdraw their letter. The Saints had not dropped their H's after all!

Best Thing for To-day	
SAINTS TO WIN	IF IT'S TRIERS———
AND	**SAINTS HAVE 'EM**
ALF. CRITCHLEY	IF IT'S TRIES———
FOR A PLAICE	**ALF. GETS 'EM**
Genuine Good Things Daily from Alf. Critchley's Quality Shops	BUT——IF IT SWIMS———
FISH—RABBITS—POULTRY	**ALF'S GOT IT**

As his advertisements show, Alf Critchley, the Saints' Committeeman and fish merchant had quite a sense of humour. A typical example of his wit could be heard after Saints had lost at Oldham in January 1930.

The stations at Oldham were Werneth, Central and Mumps.
The latter was the station tor Watersheddings.
Alf got in a tramcar after the match, and when the conductor came he said "Here lad, give us a ticket to measles and let me know when we get there".

Battle of the Giants

Despite the presence of the three H's, the record 37,169 crowd saw both defences dominate from the start. It was rare for any player to travel more than five yards with the ball without being clattered unceremoniously to the turf. The breakthrough came for Wigan from the first scrum of the second half. Binks kicked through for Sherrington to follow up and touch down for a try which Sullivan failed to convert.

It was left to the old firm of Groves and Fairclough to retreive the situation for the Saints. Wigan heeled the ball near their own line, but 'Plodder' Groves — belying his nickname, shot through and snatched the ball from his opposite number — Binks. He made a terrific burst and attempted to dive headlong through the Wigan defenders. As he was falling, he threw a low pass to the supporting Fairclough who flung himself over the line. Lewis converted to give the Saints a 5 - 3 lead, though shortly afterwards 'Plodder' blotted his copybook when he was penalized after a scuffle with the Wigan forwards. Sullivan gratefully kicked the goal for the Riversiders, and the match finished level at 5 - 5.

Wigan were not allowed the same amount of scrum possession in the replay at Leigh. Saints' veteran hooker — Bill Clarey, produced a steady stream of ball for Groves and Fairclough to get their three-quarters moving. The Saints went on to score four fabulous tries in a crushing 22 - 10 victory. The third try was undoubtedly the pick of the bunch. Groves burst through on half-way and passed to Fairclough. He swerved and left Abram for dead, glided past Parker and Kinnear and threw out a long pass for the inevitable Ellaby to take knee high and race over the line.

Back in St. Helens, the cock-a-hoop Saints tucked into a special victory tea of steak and chips at the Royal Raven Hotel. Although the toast was to Wembley, there was the sobering thought of having to clear a glut of league fixtures before the final itself. The Committee gave the team every incentive to do well, with the offer of a juicy £10 bonus for finishing in the top four – to go with the £7.10s.0d. for reaching Wembley.

More importantly, the Committee came to an agreement with the New Zealanders by making grants in lieu of the special occupations they had agreed to provide for the players. According to the Minutes of the Committee, it was resolved that:–

> *"Compensation be £4 per week, starting at once; that each player be paid £50 at once; £50 at Christmas and £50 each succeeding Christmas until each player had received the sum of £250. Each player to be guaranteed work at £3.10s.0d. per week, or work wages to be made up to this".*

A Saturday afternoon spent watching this St. Helens team packed with so many great players – was a welcome bonus in itself for many thousands of spectators who could forget about the misery of the depression, with dole queues and poverty much in evidence at the time. Indeed Alf Ellaby could always tell when it was three-quarter time at Knowsley Road because of the increase in the cheering after the unemployed had been admitted.

It proved to be quite a hard slog in those hard-baked grounds in the Spring of 1930, but the side won every one of the remaining league matches before Wembley.

They finished top of the table and secured the Lancashire League Leaders' Trophy for good measure. The 'Team of all the Talents' looked set to reap an even greater harvest of success before the end of the campaign.

The original Saints' team for the Semi-Final after the dropping of the Kiwi 'H Bombs':–

Crooks, Carr, Lewis (Capt.), Mercer, Ellaby, Fairclough, Groves, Arkwright, Clarey, Houghton, Halfpenny, Hill, Harrison.

Reserves: Turner, R. E. Jones.

CHALLENGE CUP SEMI-FINAL
Saturday, 29th March, 1930
At Station Road, Swinton
ST. HELENS (0)5 WIGAN (0)5

ST. HELENS: C. Crooks, R. Hardgrave, G. Lewis (Capt.) 1G, W. Mercer, A. Ellaby, L. Fairclough 1T, W. Groves, L. Houghton,

The Team of All The Talents (1930 — 1932)

L. Hutt, J. Arkwright, T. Hall, B. Halfpenny, R. Harrison.

WIGAN: Sullivan (Capt.) 1G, Ring, Parker, Kinnear, Brown, Binks, Abrams, Stephens, Beetham, Hodder, Mason, Dixon, Sherrington 1T.

Referee: Mr. Robinson (Bradford)
Attendance: 37,169 (Ground Record)
Receipts: £2,666

CHALLENGE CUP SEMI-FINAL REPLAY
Wednesday, 2nd April, 1930
At Mather Lane, Leigh
ST. HELENS (10)22   WIGAN (0)10

ST. HELENS: C. Crooks, R. Hardgrave, G. Lewis (Capt.) 5G, W. Mercer 1T, A. Ellaby 2T, L. Fairclough, W. Groves, L. Houghton, W. Clarey, L. Hutt 1T, B. Halfpenny, R. Harrison.

WIGAN: Sullivan (Capt.) 2G, Ring 1T, Parker, Kinnear, Brown, Binks, Abrams, Stephens, Beetham 1T, Hodder, Mason Dixon, Sherrington.

Referee: Mr. Robinson (Bradford)
Attendance: 24,000 (Ground Record)
Receipts: £1,600

PART TWO — A ROTTEN HARVEST

The Long Arm of the Law

On the Saturday before Wembley, St. Helens embarked upon the second leg of their Spring treble with a home game against Leeds in the Championship Semi-Final. The 17,000 spectators were confident of success, especially when they learned that the Loiners were missing several first team regulars through injury. The Leeds team had an unusual look about it, in more ways than one. Stan Smith — England's left winger, had been left out by the Leeds Committee and replaced by Jenkins, who was normally a second row forward. The motive was painfully obvious — to stop the Saints' danger man — Alf Ellaby at all costs!

For the next eighty minutes 'Policeman' Jenkins was never more than jersey touching reach of Alf either side of the touchline. Every time the ball went in Ellaby's direction, the 'Long arm of the Law' would hold him back and prevent him from getting into a position to accept a pass. Twice in the first half and three times in the second, Jenkins put Ellaby out of action. Three times the touch judge intervened on Ellaby's behalf, yet Bradford referee Robinson was remarkably lenient. All Jenkins received was a solitary caution for his persistent and blatant obstruction.

You have surely heard of Ellaby,
The man who nearly flies.
Though chased by Sheiks from Araby,
He keeps on scoring tries.

Dubious Leeds tactics apart, St. Helens struggled to find their form in the first half. Several times the Saints' three-quarters had the line at their mercy only for the vital pass to be dropped or intercepted. Meanwhile, at the other end — two uncharacteristic errors by Crooks and Groves let in the visitors for two converted tries to give them a surprise 10 - 0 interval lead.

There was another cruel blow for Saints' hopes ten minutes into the second half, following a melee between both sets of forwards. Fearing a repeat of the trouble at Headingley a few months earlier, referee Robinson sent off the nearest forward to him when he arrived on the scene. The crowd howled with derision as Trevor Hall, very much an innocent party – trudged disbelievingly back to the dressing room.

The Saints tried in vain to save the match, but could only manage two tries by Mercer and Hardgrave – both in the corners. Lewis failed with the conversions, and St. Helens slumped to a shock defeat. They would have conceded Leeds their ten points lead and still have won handsomely but for 'Policeman' Jenkins. Never before had it been known for a St. Helens crowd to cheer in unanimous delight if a player happened to get knocked out but, when Jenkins was momentarily stunned near the end of the game, the whole of the popular side cheered as one man – not for anything violent or dirty he had done, simply for the meanness of his deliberate obstructive methods on their idol Ellaby.

Alf's Father – Oliver, advised his son to give up the game which offered so little protection. Alf – ever the true sportsman, simply shrugged off the whole business, as did League Secretary John Wilson. "While admitting that Jenkins might have been guilty of obstructing" – he maintained, "it was the referee's duty to keep an eye on infringements, but he only cautioned Jenkins once". That – of course, was the whole trouble in the eyes of the seething St. Helens spectators.

The stage was now set for the Saints to collect the consolation prize – a Wembley win for the first time in the club's history.

"Van Ruined"

Saints' Wembley opponents were Widnes, who had reached the final somewhat unexpectedly by beating Barrow 10 - 3 in the other semi-final at Wilderspool. They included twelve Widnes-born players in their ranks, plus the thirty-seven year old South African prop George 'Tiny' Van Rooyen, who had created such an impression at Knowsley Road in the first game of the season. The Chemics had finished their league campaign in mid-table, fifteen places below St. Helens. Naturally, Jim May was confident of success as his team left for its London headquarters on the Wednesday. He said proudly:—

> *"The Saints are the best team in the league at the moment. If Widnes fulfil their promise of trying to beat us with better football, then we shall win".*

A trip to Wembley was an expensive novelty in those depressed times, and although Saints and Widnes fans poured into the stadium, the crowd of 36,544 was smaller than the previous year. Perhaps the local nature of the game appealed less to the neutral spectator than the prospect of an inter-county clash. In spite of this, when the two captains — Paddy Douglas of Widnes and Saints' George Lewis — led their teams out, side by side into the sunlit arena, the roar was deafening — very much in the Wembley tradition as we know it today.

Widnes may have been the underdogs, but that did not stop Abe Duffy, one of their most fervent supporters, from indulging in a spot of oneupmanship. He promptly scaled an upright, planting his black and white beret at the top of the post, to tremendous cheers! Paddy Douglas won the toss for the eighth match in succession and decided to play towards the goal on which the beret had been placed. As it turned out, all the Widnes points were scored at that end.

Both teams appeared slightly nervous at the outset and it was Widnes who nearly opened the scoring when a drop goal by Douglas flew just wide of the post. The blue shirted Saints were hoping to attack down both flanks, and from one such move on the right, Alf Ellaby kicked ahead. The ball passed over the line, and Peter Topping — the Widnes full-back, failed to hold it to touch down. It went a yard to one side where Lou Houghton was on hand to score for the favourites. George Lewis missed the conversion, but the Saints' supporters waited confidently for a big score to follow.

Far from collapsing, Widnes — inspired by some barnstorming runs from Van Rooyen, roared back into the game after ten minutes. Centre Albert Ratcliffe cut through the Saints' defence and put in a neat little grubber kick under the posts. This time Charlie Crooks, the St. Helens fullback, failed to gather and as 'Racker' went for the simplest of chances, Crooks obstructed him. Referee Peel was right on the spot and awarded an obstruction try which Hoey converted. Remarkably, the Chemics were in the lead!

Nothing was going right for the Saints, especially when George Lewis missed two penalties for offside, either of which would have put them back on level terms and calmed jangling nerves.

Widnes now responded to the roar of encouragement from their supporters, and put the Saints' defence under considerable pressure. In the thirty-third minute they quite deservedly went further ahead. Lewis had to play the ball near the posts, and lost possession to Millington. The young loose-forward scooped the ball up to Ratcliffe, who threw a splendid pass for winger Dennett to go in at the corner. Hoey missed the conversion, but a minute before half-time Ratcliffe made amends with a towering penalty goal to give Widnes a sensational 10 - 3 interval lead.

The bewildered St. Helens team tried desperately to redress the balance in the second half, but found the going increasingly tough. Les Fairclough — the pivot of so many attacking moves from stand-off half, was tightly marked by his opposite number — Jerry Laughton, and showed only glimpses of his true form. As the game entered its final quarter, the Widnes line had several close escapes. The flying Ellaby got loose twice, and each time there were cries of "He's over" from the St. Helens faithful. But the Widnes cover defence in which Peter Topping was outstanding held firm, and was never seriously threatened again until referee Peel blew for full-time.

ST. HELENS – WIDNES 1930 RLCC FINAL
COMPARISON OF TEAMS

ST. HELENS

Name	Age	Height	Weight
C. Crooks	33	5' 10"	11.02
A. Ellaby	26	6' 0"	13.00
W. Mercer	24	5' 8"	11.00
G. Lewis	29	5' 8"	11.06
R. A. Hardgrave	22	5' 7"	10.12
L. Fairclough	26	5' 7"	10.10
W. Groves	33	5' 9"	12.00
L. Hutt	24	6' 0"	14.00
W. Clarey	30	5' 11"	13.00
L. Houghton	25	5' 11"	13.04
E. T. Hall	24	6' 1"	13.06
B. Halfpenny	26	6' 0"	13.04
R. Harrison	22	5' 9"	12.06

WIDNES

Name	Age	Height	Weight
R. Fraser	22	5' 10"	12.03
J. Dennett	21	5' 8"	10.10
A. Ratcliffe	25	5' 8"	12.00
P. Topping	20	5' 6"	10.10
H. Owen	22	5' 6"	10.00
J. Laughton	25	5' 8"	11.11
P. Douglas	27	5' 5"	10.08
F. Kelsall	23	6' 1"	14.08
G. Stevans	28	5' 10"	12.08
N. Silcock	26	5' 11½"	14.02
G. Van Rooyen	37	6' 2¼"	16.00
J. Hoey	26	6' 0"	13.05
H. Millington	21	5' 9"	12.08

Back in St. Helens, those supporters who were listening to the match report on the radio, could hardly believe their ears as the full-time score crackled through the old horn type loudspeakers .... Widnes 10 – St. Helens 3. It was incredible, but it was true!

The Saints and their supporters watched in dismay as Paddy Douglas was carried shoulder high across the field to receive the Challenge Cup from Lord Lonsdale. To set the seal on a thoroughly miserable day, it later transpired that the players' wives had not even seen the match. They had left St. Helens in a motor coach in the early hours of the morning, and with a breakdown en route – had arrived at the stadium to hear the final whistle sounding. By the time they got inside, the players had gone to the dressing rooms and the inquests were just beginning.

If the Saints had shown their true form and had still been beaten, their supporters would not have felt so sad. 'Premier' wrote:–

"No-one had seen the real St. Helens team; the team of speed, strength and combination, the team of perfect backing-up, the team of irresistible dash and determination".

Although bitterly disappointed, the St. Helens' players accepted defeat graciously. They knew that the better team had won on the day. If there had been a player of the match award, the sixteen stone powerhouse Van Rooyen would have won hands down. Jim Sullivan. – who was an interested spectator said:–

"He took on the whole of St. Helens that day and licked them. Afterwards, I met him outside Wembley and I've never seen a man so battered and weary – but so happy!"

Indeed Van Rooyen could have been holding his winner's medal as a St. Helens player. When he was up for transfer at the start of the 1927-28 season, the Saints' Committee put in an offer which was way below Wigan's asking price of £300 and nothing came of it.

Van Rooyen apart, there is little doubt that the Saints were beaten largely by what they had gone through before they reached Wembley, a view held by the great Alf Ellaby some fifty-five years hence:–

"Widnes were by far the better side, don't get me wrong, but it was also the stupidity of the Committee that lost us the match. We left St. Helens on Wednesday and stayed at the Palace Hotel in Bloomsbury. Thursday was a boiling hot day and they took us for a walk on Hampstead Heath. In the evening we went to a show at the Dominion Theatre in Oxford Street and got to bed at midnight. On Friday morning we went to Wembley and they had us running about on the field to get used to it. I said to George Lewis – "they're killing us you know". The MP for St. Helens invited us to visit the Houses of Parliament on Friday evening. We had dinner and set off. We walked from Bloomsbury Square through Aldwych, along the Strand, down Whitehall to the Houses of Parliament. We even visited the cellars. George

The Team of All The Talents (1930 – 1932)

Lewis thought we were looking for Guy Fawkes' nephew! Anyhow, they walked us back and we were in our beds on the eve of the match for half-past-one".

In the first few minutes of the game, I got a ball from George Lewis with only the full-back to beat, and when I got to him I kicked. Why? Beacuse I was jiggered. Normally I would not have looked at him on my way to the line. It was pure luck that the ball ended up in Lou Houghton's hands for him to score. I said to George Lewis at half-time — "We can't win, we're jiggered". He agreed.

To show you how good a side we really were — we came back on the Monday, did nothing all week, played Wigan on the Saturday and beat them thirty points to something. Why? — because we rested. You can't start a car on a low battery. We left our energy on the streets of London".

Alf Ellaby never fulfilled his ambition of owning a Challenge Cup winner's medal, and it was forty-six years before the Saints had a chance to avenge their shock defeat by meeting their adversaries in the 1976 Final. Widnes were the favourite team, the Saints an ageing side — ripe for the slaughter. On that sun-baked afternoon 'Dad's Army' wiped the slate clean with a 20 - 5 victory — all part of that glorious uncertainty that makes a Wembley Final so special.

WITH THEIR CHINS OUT LIKE WINNERS!
"Express" Cartoon of Saints' Cup Final Team

St. Helens Newspaper, Friday, May 2nd. 1930

CHALLENGE CUP FINAL
Saturday, 3rd May, 1930
At Wembley Stadium
ST. HELENS (3)3   WIDNES (10)10

The Team of All The Talents (1930 — 1932)

ST. HELENS: C. Crooks, A. Ellaby, W. Mercer, G. Lewis (Capt.), R. Hardgrave, L. Fairclough, W. Groves, L. Hutt, W. Clarey, L. Houghton 1T, T. Hall, B. Halfpenny, R. Harrison.

WIDNES: R. Frazer, J. Dennett 1T, A. Ratcliffe 1T, 1G, P. Topping, H. Owen, P. Douglas (Capt.), J. Laughton, F. Kelsall, G. Stevens, N. Silcock, G. Van Rooyen, H. Millington, J. Hoey 1G.

Referee: Mr. Peel (Bradford)
Attendance 36,544
Receipts: £3,102

PART THREE — T' BEST IN THE NORTHERN UNION

The Saints nearly made a quick return to Wembley in 1930-31, only to be beaten 11 - 2 by the eventual winners — Halifax in the Semi-Final at Rochdale. League form was also disappointing in spite of some fine contributions from Ellaby and Hardgrave, who scored forty-three and thirty-three tries respectively. Injuries to key players at critical times was a major factor. Trevor Hall had been particularly unlucky and returned to New Zealand with Lou Hutt at the end of the season.

The Recs won the Lancashire Cup in grand style by beating Wigan 18 - 3 at Swinton, but there was no winners medal for international forward — Albert Fildes. He had been 'canonized' beforehand and was now a Saint! The Committee had long admired his terrific tackling and were delighted to see him in a red and white jersey at last. One Recs supporter remarked:—

"Yet when they got him, they were soon proudly boasting that they had taught him to play football. His trump suit was how to stop it".

Fildes — the landlord of the White Lion in Church Street, formed part of a formidable pack in 1931-32, which also included his fellow Tourist from 1928 — Ben Halfpenny. One of the rising stars of the forwards however, was Jack Arkwright. He had suffered the biggest disappointment of his career after being left out of the Wembley team two years before. He said later:—

"I got on my motor-bike which I bought with part of my signing on fee, and rode home with tears in my eyes".

Arkwright was well over six feet tall, extremely fast for his size and a formidable figure to tackle in full flight with his knees-up running style. George Lewis remembers him putting this to good effect in a match against Leigh:—

"I kicked off at the start of the match. Arkie chased after the ball, caught it in one of his shovel-like hands and dived under the posts for one of the quickest tries on record. Unfortunately, Jack also had a bit of a temper. He got laid out at Bradford one day and we had to walk him round to revive him. When he came to, he kept asking me to "kick it to yon feller". I daren't — otherwise Jack would have probably been sent off".

Another surprise addition to the pack was Walter Groves, who had shared a successful benefit the previous season with Les Fairclough. His rough and ready style proved ideal for the loose-forward role. Walter might have been a hard man but, according to Billy Greenall, he had a heart of gold:—

"In my first match for the Recs against Saints, Walter was my opposing scrum-half. After the first scrummage he came to me, put his arm round my shoulder and asked if anyone was knocking me about. I said "no". "Tell me if they do lad" — he said, "I don't care who it is — if they

bother you they'll be sorry!" That happened every time I played against him. He would walk off the field with his arm over my shoulder".

The club was lucky to have ready made replacements for Groves and the injured Les Fairclough in scrum-half Harry Frodsham, brother of Alf, and Jack Garvey — a fine stand-off half, quick as lightning over thirty yards. Tom Winnard had been signed as a utility back from Wigan Highfield and played mostly in the centre with Billy Mercer. Winnard was a 'rag and bone man' from Wigan. When he signed for St. Helens, Bill Simister took one look at his scruffy appearance and decided to give him a suit to smarten him up. Winnard took it home and promptly sold it!

That old stalwart Charlie Crooks had retired and George Lewis filled the vacant full-back berth, while on the flanks Ellaby and Hardgrave were the scourge of every defence with their devastating finishing.

In 1931-32 Hardgrave scored forty-four tries to Ellaby's thirty-three, almost the reverse of the previous season — as the Saints clinched second place in the table and lifted the Lancashire League trophy. They won the last ten league games in succession, and the little Kiwi equalled Ellaby's feat of 1926-27 of scoring tries in nine consecutive club games in March and April, 1932.

The Saints faced the Championship Semi-Final at home to Leeds without Ellaby and Fildes, who had been selected to tour Australia and New Zealand once again with the Rugby League Lions. Bob Jones — normally a centre, had replaced Ellaby on the wing, and the 14,000 spectators were relieved to see that there would be no repetition of the Jenkins fiasco, as Leeds had selected two bona-fide wingers!

In a dour first half, the Leeds marking was a little over-enthusiastic and referee Peel penalized them frequently for off-side. Lewis and Winnard each kicked a penalty goal to give St. Helens a 4 - 0 half-time lead which they just about deserved.

After the break, the Saints continually pounded the Leeds line and, in one such assault, George Lewis kicked through and followed up to hustle his opposite number — Brough. The Leeds man failed to gather and the ball broke to Arkwright, who picked up and ran like a trojan ten yards along the touch-line with three men on him and scored at the flag. Two Leeds forwards had charged sideways at him but could not put him in touch. Winnard failed with the conversion, but a minute later Leeds were again caught off-side at a scrum. Lewis kicked a splendid goal to send the jubilant Saints into their first ever Championship final, and the chance of a memorable two-trophy haul.

Saints at the Double

Huddersfield — those great title chasers, were Saints' opponents in the final at Wakefield on 7th May. Nearly 2,000 St. Helens' supporters had crossed the Pennines and gave a huge roar as the Red and Whites ran out on to the Belle Vue turf. St. Helens won the toss, and George Lewis decided to play with the wind in their favour in the first half. Unfortunately, Tom Winnard failed to take advantage and missed two early penalty attempts. Another chance went begging as Roy Hardgrave went in at the corner, following excellent work by Mercer — but he had put a foot in touch.

Despite these setbacks, persistent pressure by the Saints was soon to have its reward. Garvey got the ball from a scrum and shot through the flat-footed Yorkshire defence. He swerved round full-back Bowkett and as second rower Tiffany tried a desperate cover tackle, flipped the ball to Winnard in a superb demonstration of the scissors move and the centre scored a gem of a try in the corner, which was converted by Lewis.

Huddersfield did their utmost to get in the game, but to no avail. George Lewis in particular was rock-solid at full-back and an inspiration to his team mates. Just before half-time, Winnard found touch near the Huddersfield line and scrum-half Thompson was penalized for feeding. Lewis piloted the ball over the bar to give the Saints a seven point lead.

During the interval, two Saints supporters got into earnest conversation with two hefty looking fellows supporting Huddersfield. "We don't mind this lot with their bits of obstruction" they were saying, "it's teams like Leeds we can't stick with their so-and-so's like Jenkins on the wing".

"You'll excuse me" — said the smaller of their two opponents, "but my friend here happens to be Jenkins — and I'm Rosser!"

Thankfully the Headingley Welshmen saw the funny side and good humour prevailed as the second half began.

Bowkett soon registered Huddersfield's first points with a drop-goal, but Lewis replied with another well taken penalty after Garvey had been obstructed following a kick ahead. The St. Helens defence seemed to be coping admirably until Jones and Lewis let a high ball bounce between them and Walker rushed in to score for Huddersfield. Bowkett missed the conversion and there was no further scoring in the match.

The last ten minutes had been agony for Saints' Committeeman — Bill Simister. The milk dealer from Cornwall who was always a nervous spectator, had spent the time groaning with his head in his hands, fearing the worst. He had brightened up considerably however, when George Lewis was presented with the trophy by the League Secretary — Mr. J. W. Wood. Lewis could not easily be seen by the triumphant St. Helens' supporters, but Big 'Arkie' soon put that right! He took hold of his Captain and with one solid heave put him and the Cup safely on his broad shoulders.

As soon as the team returned to St. Helens — they boarded an open motor coach and drove to Harry Ince's house. The former Secretary, who was seriously ill, stood at his bedroom window with tears in his eyes as George Lewis showed him the Cup and his team mates sang their victory hymn 'Praise God from Whom all Blessings Flow'.

The Mayor — Alderman Hewitt, welcomed back the new League Champions in front of a wildly enthusiastic crowd in the Town Hall Square. Half an hour later, the team boarded their coach for a tour of the town with George Lewis in front proudly holding the silverware. It certainly had been a memorable benefit season for the Saints' skipper! Needless to say, the party ended up at the White Lion Hotel, where the Cup was filled over and over again in triumph, and hundreds must have had enormous 'sups' out of it.

The following day at St. Andrews Church in Dentons Green, Saints' supporters in the congregation smiled broadlly as they sang a line from Psalm 149 — 'Let the Saints be joyful with glory'. What could have been more appropriate!

LEAGUE CHAMPIONSHIP FINAL
Saturday, 7th May, 1932
At Belle Vue, Wakefield
ST. HELENS (7)9   HUDDERSFIELD (0)5

ST. HELENS: G. Lewis (Capt.) 3G, R. Hardgrave, W. Mercer, T. Winnard 1T, R. E. Jones, H. Frodsham, J. Garvey, R. Atkin, D. Cotton, E. Hill, B. Halfpenny, J. Arkwright, W. Groves.

HUDDERSFIELD: Bowkett 1G, Mills, Parker, Walshaw, Walker 1T, Thompson, Richards, Rudd, Halliday, Sherwood, Tiffany, Banks, Young.

Referee: Mr. Fairhurst (Wigan)
Attendance: 20,000
Receipts: £1,980

Chapter 9
Survival of the Fittest (1933 − 1939)

Going to the Dogs

Some weeks after the championship success, came news of further glory for the St. Helens Tourists in Australia − and Alf Ellaby in particular. 'Wallaby' scored a sensational interception try in the first test at Sydney in front of a World record 70,000 crowd and made another for Atkinson, as Great Britain held on for an 8 - 6 victory. Although the Kangaroos tied the series with a 15 - 6 win at Brisbane a fortnight later, Fildes joined Ellaby for the crucial final test at Sydney on 16th July. Britain roared back from a 9 - 0 deficit to win 18 - 15 and retain the Ashes.

The two Saints appeared together in all but one of the test matches against New Zealand on the second leg of the tour. Britain won all three in grand style. Ellaby and Fildes returned to Britain proud to have been associated with one of the happiest and most successful tours ever undertaken 'Down Under'.

They might well have come back to see several changes had taken place at the Knowsley Road ground during the summer. Chairman − Syd Morris and his Committee, ever mindful of mounting financial pressures − had explored the possibility of letting the ground for greyhound racing. According to the Minutes of the Committee, the St. Helens Greyhound Stadium Company Limited had agreed to pay the club £50 per year for the use of the ground, £250 per year for the use of the stands and turnstiles, plus 10% of the profits. It was even decided where the totalizators and kennels should be built on the ground.

There was much opposition to the proposed plans especially from religious groups in the town. The Rev. Canon Child resigned his position as Hon. Club Chaplain when the proposals reached the press. Yet the development never took place. It contravened the covenant of the deed under which the club had purchased the ground and pavilion from Pilkington Brothers back in 1925.

At the time £2,500 was advanced on mortgage by Mr. Sam Robinson of Greenalls to effect the purchase, and a Ground Redemption Fund was opened − into which certain amounts were placed for payment of interest and capital.

It was ironical that in spite of the highest ever league position at the end of 1931-32, revenue was the lowest for several seasons. Treasurer George Boardman blamed the depression for the lack of a 'Championship profit'. The financial situation showed no signs of improving as the 1932-33 season got under way, and Greenall Whitley gave a further loan of £1,000 to alleviate the overdraft at the bank. The players were forced — rather reluctantly, to accept a reduction in wages. At the meeting where this was discussed, George Lewis asked the Committee if the cuts would be made up with bonuses in Cup Ties. The Chairman refused to make any comment!

Even so, it did not stop the Saints from blazing a victory trail in the Lancashire Cup, starting with a magnificent win at Widnes in the first round. Broughton and Salford were beaten to clinch a place in the final against Warrington at Wigan. There was plenty of action for the 28,500 spectators crammed into Central Park. St. Helens went in at half-time 7 - 5 ahead, thanks to a Fildes try and two goals from Lewis. The cover tackling of Fildes and Arkwright in the second row was magnificent, especially when the Warrington centres Shankland and Dingsdale threatened to over-run their St. Helens counterparts.

Unfortunately, both forwards picked up knocks early in the second half, which hampered their effectiveness. The Warrington three-quarters took full advantage and Dingsdale put winger Thompson in for a try which Holding converted to ease the Wirepullers into a 9 - 6 lead. George Lewis kicked a penalty goal, and the stage was set for a thrilling finale.

The last chance of all came when the Saints were swarming all over the Warrington line and a defender kicked the ball out to the twenty-five. Fullback Bob Jones was in a good position to take it, right in front of the posts — with his nearest opponent at least fifteen yards away. The St. Helens supporters roared at him with one voice to drop a goal. He held out his arms, allowed the ball to get a fraction on the low side and had to make a second movement to control it. He hesitated slightly and then turned his face to the corner flag and booted the ball straight to Thompson — who fielded, punched it vigorously to half way and it was all over.

Shankland collected the trophy for the Wires as the Saints' supporters drifted away to drown their sorrows. Everyone agreed that had Winnard and Mercer not been missing, and Arkwright and Fildes not been hurt it would have been a different story.

LANCASHIRE CUP FINAL
Saturday, 19th November, 1932
At Central Park, Wigan
ST. HELENS (7)9   WARRINGTON (5)10

ST. HELENS: R. E. Jones, R. Hardgrave, A. Butler, G. Lewis (Capt.) 3G, A. Ellaby, J. Garvey, H. Frodsham, D. Cotton, R. Atkin, B. Halfpenny, A. Fildes 1T, J. Arkwright, W. Groves.
WARRING-TON: Holding 2G, Thompson 1T, Dingsdale, Shankland (Capt.) Ray, Oster, Davies 1T, Miller, Bentham, Hardman, Jones, Evans, Seeling.
Referee: Mr. Brown
Attendance: 28,500
Receipts: £1,675

Gates continued to fall in the bleak winter of 1932, and by New Year the Committee had no option but to do what Frank McCormick had done ten years earlier — approach the public for financial support. There was a ready response from the sportsmen of the town, which resulted in the inauguration of a Million Penny Fund — by the Mayor — Councillor T. Wood. A Special Committee was formed, and several schemes launched by them towards the attainment of the fund's objective.

Despite the difficulties, the Committee were reluctant to relieve the financial burden by selling any star players, especially when the team embarked upon a promising Challenge Cup run in February. Bradford were beaten 24 - 3 away in the first round, and Hunslet fell 14 - 3 at Knowsley Road in the second. Another home tie saw St. Helens march into the semi-finals at the expense of Halifax.

By a strange coincidence their opponents in the semi-final were Warrington once again, and over 30,000 at Swinton waited to see if the Saints could avenge their County Cup defeat.

Before the kick-off, the Committee caused quite a sensation by leaving out Captain and goal kicker George Lewis. To make matters worse, he was later refused entry into the grandstand — as those same Committeemen looked on seemingly unconcerned. Alf Ellaby captained the side in his absence, although he was carrying an injury himself and was far from being fully fit.

Both teams scored a try apiece, with Ellaby touching down for the Saints, but the major difference in a close encounter was the goal kicking. The Committee's gamble had failed and Lewis's marksmanship was sorely missed. Full-back Billy Holding kicked four goals to Tom Winnard's one — as Warrington rubbed salt into the wound by winning 11 - 5.

It was a disappointing finish to the season for Alf Ellaby in his benefit year. He — like so many St. Helens supporters who trudged dejectedly away from Station Road, had a feeling that the great period of success was coming to an end.

The End of an Era

The team of all the talents began to break up in 1933-34. Les Fairclough was forced to give up the game with a knee injury after several unsuccessful comeback attempts in the 'A' team. Walter Groves had retired, Tom Winnard was transferred to Bradford Northern and Roy Hardgrave returned to New Zealand at the end of the season, although he later came back to play for York. The Saints finished in thirteenth place in the League — their lowest position for nearly a decade, and were knocked out of the cup by unfancied Bramley in the second round at Barley Mow.

Faced with declining gates and a high wages bill, the Committee had no option but to consider offers for some of their star players. Early in the close season Jack Garvey — the local boy who had developed into one of the best half-backs in Lancashire — went to Broughton Rangers. Worse was to come at the end of July when the Committee accepted £800 from Wigan for Alf Ellaby. The money spelt financial security for the Saints who were perilously close to bankruptcy.

Ellaby was landlord of the Veevers Arms in Blackpool at the time and was sorry to leave his home town club in such circumstances after so many years of success. He could have joined Broughton, but refused.

"I told the Broughton Directors that even if I did sign for them there was no guarantee I was going to get the ball. A winger may as well draw social security without it. Wigan were the only other club I would have played for. They always had a good side who moved the ball out wide, which suited me down to the ground".

Ellaby was getting towards the end of his career, but played many grand games for Wigan in his three year stay, scoring eighty tries. George Lewis maintained:—

"The club was never the same after Alf went. The following Good Friday he scored a try against us — and was positively apologetic about it! His heart was not really in the Wigan club".

After Ellaby had gone, the Committee decided to try and build a team round the mighty frame of Jack Arkwright. He did not fancy the idea however, and was put on the transfer list at the start of 1934-35 season. He signed for Warrington for £800 and became one of the greatest second row forwards of his time — at home and abroad, until his retirement in 1939.

Starting Over

By 1935 the break up was complete. Most of the big names from three years before had been either transferred or retired from the game. The Committee were determined to start building a new team, though with somewhat limited resources. A number of new players joined the club, including the biggest influx of Welshmen since the early 1920's.

Among the first was Arthur Lemon, a Welsh rugby union international forward from Neath — in the twilight of his career. Now Arthur liked the odd glass of beer and could not believe his luck when he got a job at Greenalls as a carpenter. He wrote a letter home to his Father, telling him of his newly found employment. "I believe the old chap's not stopped laughing yet" — he told George Lewis a few weeks later.

Lewis remembers one occasion when Arthur arrived late for training, a little worse for wear having had a right skinful that afternoon. Ted Forber ordered him to do six laps of the field, which was positively unheard of. Old Arthur went round like an express train. "What else can I do George, but report him fit" — said the exasperated Saints trainer.

Les Fairclough 'The Little Drummer Boy'

Season	Club Apps	Tries	Goals	Gt. Britain Apps	Tries	England Apps	Tries	Lancashire Apps	Tries	GB Tour Apps	Tries
1920/21	10	1									
1921/22	23	6									
1922/23	37	5									
1923/24	30	11	1					1			
1924/25	36	7	1			1		2	1		
1925/26	35	9				2	1	2	1		
1926/27	37	17		1	1	1	1	1			
1927/28	31	10				1		3			
1928 Tour				4	5					8	6
1928/29	30	6				1		3	2		
1929/30	38	5	1	1		1		3	1		
1930/31	34	5				2		3			
1931/32	9	2						2			
1932/33	2										
Totals	352	84	3	6	6	9	2	20	5	8	6

George Lewis 'Points Machine'

Season	Club Apps	Tries	Goals	Wales Apps	Tries	Monmouthshire App	Tries	Goals	Glamorgan & Monmouthshire Apps	Tries
1921/22	4	1	2							
1922/23	38	12	73							
1923/24	36	1	75							
1924/25	36	6	64							
1925/26	31	5	65							
1926/27	41	4	107*	2		1	1	1		
1927/28	34	5	67						2	
1928/29	30	3	57							
1929/30	47	1	83						1	
1930/31	37	2	76							
1931/32	36	4	78							
1932/33	36	0	74							
1933/34	9	0	10							
1934/35	13	0	16							
1935/36	1	0	2							
Totals:	429	44	849	2		1	1	1	3	

* First century of goals kicked by a St Helens player in a season.

One of Lemon's former team mates in Wales — loose-forward Ossie Griffiths, was signed from Wigan and shortly afterwards Bert Jones — a twenty-two year old international scrum-half from Neath, threw in his lot with the Saints. Unfortunately, he did not settle down in the new code and went back home after thirteen matches. Others included Islwyn (Izzy) Davies, the Swansea and Glamorgan winger who made a name for himself and then joined Warrington — and Ossie Jones, a centre from Neath.

The Welsh connection continued when George Lewis was appointed coach for a spell in the mid-thirties. He signed a young lad from a junior team in Pontypool, called Stan Powell — who became first choice stand-off half at nineteen. Meanwhile, Lewis's old comrade Trevor Hall rejoined the club, and Jackie Bradbury — a utility-back was snapped up from Bradford Northern. Yet in spite of the new blood, the Saints celebrated their Diamond Jubilee in 1935-36 as a second class outfit, floundering in the lower half of the table.

Going Public

St. Helens struggled through the 1936-37 season with more poor results and gates down to 2,000 at Knowsley Road. The club finished in the lower reaches of the league and had to rely on the holiday matches against Wigan and Recs to bring in much-needed revenue. Former loose-forward Arthur Cross maintains that they were so hard up they were desperate to play those games whatever the conditions — bone hard pitch or not!

The glory days may well have disappeared but, according to Arthur's second row colleague Ted Beesley, they were happy times:—

"George Lewis was coach when I signed from the Junior League. Training consisted of laps round the pitch and then we did sprints behind the grandstand. The session ended with a game of touch rugby. A fellow named Joe Carson from Dentons Green was our trainer — he had thin bony fingers which felt like rods of iron when he massaged you.

"Unlike today, few wore shoulder pads but shin pads were essential! At the play-the-ball, both sides could kick for it. The ankles used to get a lot of clog as well because you had to jump for the ball from every kick-off. There were some jokers too! Full-back Albert Butler who played for Lancashire was always one for pranks. One day after training, he put somebody's shirt on and starting larking about. One of the forwards called Thompson threw a bucket of water over him. Imagine the look on Thompson's face when he realised that it was his own shirt Butler was wearing!"

There were more serious matters to be discussed in the close season however.

At a public meeting on Thursday, 6th May the Mayor, Alderman Dodd, outlined plans for the formation of a Limited Liability Company:—

Survival of the Fittest (1933 — 1939)

"We shall require £2,675 to clear off the indebtedness of the Company and be able to carry on. We shall only float the Company if we receive a minimum of £4,000 and that would leave us £1,300 as a working balance with which to carry on. With a balance like that, carefully handled, we think it will be possible to carry on the club — at any rate for some time, and see whether we can get it on its feet".

By early June nearly £2,000 of the 10/- shares had been taken up, but the response from the general public was poor. A great deal of the money had been raised by the prospective Directors or members of the Organizing Committee. Also many tradespeople accepted shares as a settlement of their debts instead of pressing for liquidation and a return of their money in some measure.

As the deadline approached at the end of August, nearly 1,500 shares still had to be found. The local press appealed for people to rally round with applications for two or three shares per person in order to find the necessary capital. At the eleventh hour, help came from a most surprising source. The Rugby League took out 600 shares at a cost of £300 — the first occasion that they had taken out shares in any Company. It was a veritable shot in the arm for the club's prospects. Shortly afterwards the £4,000 target was reached and the Saints went public for the first time.

Before the start of the season, the Board of Directors — or 'Twelve Apostles' as they became known, met the players and stressed how vital improved results were for the success of the venture. On 28th August, 1937 the Saints ran out for their first match under the new regime against Widnes at Knowsley Road. They wore new jerseys with two thin red bands above and below the broad red band, which were a gift from the lady supporters.

The 4,000 crowd howled with delight when Emlyn Hughes (Uncle of the famous Liverpool and England soccer player) picked up from a melee and plunged over for St. Helens' first try. Shannon replied with a try for Widnes a few minutes later, which Topping converted to give the Chemics a two point interval lead.

In the second half St. Helens dominated the game. Prop Stan Hill scored their second try and with two minutes to go Forsyth clinched two points for the Saints. The flying winger intercepted a Widnes pass from a scrum near the touchline side and scored a glorious try in the corner.

"The old Saint has regained his halo" — wrote one critic, and certainly the early season results seemed to warrant such optimism. Winning pay at home was £3.10s.0d. and the club asked the players if they would accept a 10/- share to make up their wages. "We politely declined the Board's kind offer" said Arthur Cross, with more than a hint of sarcasm!

LEAGUE MATCH
(First as a Limited Company)

Saturday, 28th August, 1937
At Knowsley Road
ST. HELENS (3)11   WIDNES (5)7

ST. HELENS: Parkinson, Forsyth 1T, Bradbury (Capt.), Jones, Hesketh, Powell 1G, Kelly, Hill 1T, Dullard, Cuncliffe, Hughes 1T, Johnson, Beesley.

WIDNES: Bradley, White, Topping 1G, Barber, Gallimore, Shannon 1T, McCue, Silcock, Jones, Roberts, McDowell, Hoey 1G, Millington.

Referee: Mr. Harding (Broughton)
Attendance: 4,000
Receipts: £138

Alf Ellaby rejoined the club in December from Wigan, and one of Ted Beesley's biggest regrets is that he never played in the same team as his idol.

"Unfortunately I was reserve when he played his comeback match against Barrow. I've seen him score many tries from his own line. He would run up to his opponent and lose him for sheer pace — a marvellous player — although past his best when he came back to St. Helens".

Despite the great man's presence, the young Saints team faded to finish in a disappointing twenty-first place with thirty-one points. The Recs were below them in twenty-second position. It was the beginning of the end of Rugby League as people had known it in the town for the last two decades.

Alf Ellaby 'The Hat-Trick King'

Season	Club Apps	Club Tries	Great Britain Apps	Great Britain Tries	England App	England Tries	Lancs. App	Lancs. Tries	Great Britain Tour App	Great Britain Tour Tries	Great Britain Tour Goals	Rugby League XIII App	Rugby League XIII Tries
1925/26	7	9											
1926/27	41	50*			1	1	2	4					
1927/28	29	33			1	3	1						
1928 Tour			5	4					9	16	2		
1928/29	22	30			1	3	3	4					
1929/30	35	33	2				4	6					
1930/31	37	37			2	5	3	1					
1931/32	26	33			1	1	2	1					
1932 Tour			5	3					9	18			
1932/33	30	17			1		2	1					
1933/34	35	27	1				2					1	4
1937/38	24	8											
1938/39	4	1											
Totals	290	278	13	7	7	13	19	17	18	34	2	1	4

Survival of the Fittest (1933 — 1939)

* FIRST HALF-CENTURY OF TRIES IN A SEASON BY A
ST. HELENS PLAYER

HAT TRICKS:
31   for St. Helens
1   for England
1   for Rugby League XIII

Roy Hardgrave 'The Newton Flyer'

	Club		Other Nationalities	
Season	App	Tries	App	Tries
1929/30	47	33		
1930/31	41	32	1	
1931/32	42	44		
1932/33	46	34	1	1
1933/34	35	30		
Totals	211	173	2	1

St. Helens United

During the halcyon days of St. Helens Rugby League, between 1927 and 1933 — rugby followers in the town boasted that a team from the Recs and Saints could have beaten any team in the country. The production of local talent was truly at its peak and, in addition to providing two teams, there were enough St. Helens players travelling to other clubs in Lancashire and Yorkshire to have furnished another St. Helens side.

By the late thirties however, rugby league was no longer flourishing in the town, and both Saints and Recs were in decline. A measure of their fall from prominence could be seen when the fixtures for the visiting Australian Tourists were announced for 1937/38. In previous years both the local sides had matches against the Kangaroos. Times had changed. The Saints and Recs were no longer considered strong enough to face the Tourists individually, and a combined team was selected for the first and only time.

The match was played on a gloomy Thursday afternoon in December in front of less than 2,000 spectators at Knowsley Road. Beaton opened Australia's account with a penalty goal, and second rower Lewis powered through for a try to give the 'Green and Golds' an ominously early 5 - 0 lead. The St. Helens lads were made of stern stuff, however. From a scrum near the Kangaroos' line — Bradbury picked up and plunged through the opening-out scrum for a grand try. His club mate Powell's conversion hit the post and bounced over to put the St. Helens XIII on level terms at 5 - 5.

It was only in the second half that the great power of the Australians was seen to good effect, more so when the Recs pair of Eli Dixon and Ernie Large was forced to leave the field with injuries. Beaton and Williams added further tries for the Tourists, and they eventually won a thrilling contest 15 - 7.

AUSTRALIAN TOUR 1937-38
Thursday, 2nd December, 1937
At Knowsley Road
ST. HELENS XIII (5)7   AUSTRALIA (5)15

ST. HELENS: Butler (S), Bailey (R), E. Dixon (R), Fearnley (S), Large (R), Powell (S), Bradbury (S), Parr (R), Roberts (S), Dunn (R), Hughes (S), Atherton (R), Hutcheson (S).

AUSTRALIA: Whittle, Dawson, Williams, Beaton, McLean, Norman, Thompson, Pierce, Ferall, Griffiths, McLennan, Lewis, Prigg.

St. Helens Scorers: T. Bradbury
                      G. Powell (2)

Australian Scorers: T. Lewis, Beaton, Williams,
                      G. Beaton (2), Thompson

           Referee: Mr. Armstrong (Huddersfield)
        Attendance: 2,000

Town with a Tomb

Results had once again been disappointing for the Saints in 1938-39. Yet there were some promising signs for the future. Coach Oliver Dolan, the former Recs and Great Britain hooker — could call on a useful mixture of youth and experience. Among the good young prospects were Harry Briscoe — a scrum-half who had played in the first team as a sixteen year old in 1937 — and Jack Waring, a fine centre three-quarter. The club was determined to continue the search for new players and appointed a full-time scout for that purpose.

Two experienced campaigners were added to the squad before the season's end. Half-back Frank Tracey was secured from the Recs for £350 and George 'Porky' Davies — a rough and ready forward arrived from Liverpool Stanley for a fee of £275. Their transfers were unique in that the Supporters' Club had given £250 to the parent club to complete the transactions.

In the 1970's the Supporters' Club made a similar approach to the Board with regard to re-siging Ken Kelly from Bradford Northern. History did not repeat itself though, and the offer was not entertained.

142   *Survival of the Fittest (1933 — 1939)*

RUGBY LEAGUE CUP SIDELIGHTS.—BY BERT WRIGHT.

Evening Express, January 26th, 1938

The Saints were by no means clear of debt in 1939, and had to apply for an extension of their £600 overdraft at the bank. Neighbours Recs were in even more serious trouble. They had lost over £1,000 in 1938-39, and events gradually drew towards a crisis. Most clubs managed to keep going on whist drives and light entertainment, which were run by supporters who were determined to keep the game going. This was below the dignity of what essentially was the Pilkington works club, and it was decided that the Recs would have to close down. Notice of their resignation was sent to Rugby League Headquarters in April, 1939 and was accepted with regret — to take effect from 31st July, 1939.

"It was no surprise when the Recs packed up" — said Len Kilshaw. "A works team never has the same grip as the town team. No-one at the Recs

Survival of the Fittest (1933 – 1939)

could have done what Frank McCormick did to save the Saints. During the crisis at City Road there was a feeling of complacency — that Pilkington Brothers would pull them out of the soup — but it never happened!"

Alf Ellaby — who retired in 1939, thought it a great pity that the Recs had closed down. "It used to be the one topic of conversation looking forward to the Christmas games" he recalled. In fact, Alf's big break into International football came when 'Tot' Wallace the Recs winger received a knee injury and had to drop out of the England side. Ellaby was the reserve to take his place and made good use of that opportunity.

Memories of the Derby clashes between Saints and Recs are legion. Perhaps one of the most talked about concerns Tommy Smith — the Recs' forward and his famous try at Knowsley Road, when he ran straight into one of the uprights! Tommy was a tough customer though; and was soon back in the action.

The Saints played forty-seven Derby games with their old enemy, winning twenty-one, losing twenty with six draws, leaving them with a one match advantage. Much of their ascendancy however, was gained during the Recs' fading years after 1930. In points scoring, the advantage lay with the Recs — 365 against 247.

The last Derby match in the league was played at City Road on New Year's Day 1939, and ended in a 5 - 3 win for the visitors. Ted Beesley scored a try for St. Helens and Powell kicked a penalty goal. Tracey was the Recs try-scorer.

Epilogue

When the New Zealand team visited Knowsley Road on Saturday, 2nd September, 1939 for the opening match of their tour, the demise of the Recs was not exactly the biggest talking point! Germany had invaded Poland twenty-four hours earlier, and King George VI had signed an order in council mobilizing the Armed Forces.

The match itself was not a sparkling success from a rugby point of view, although Knowsley Road stalwarts who were there on that memorable day will, no doubt, recall one particular highlight. Jones — the tall Kiwi forward, and Fearnley the Saints' skipper — raced neck and neck for a ball lying beyond the try line. The New Zealander's extra height helped him in his thrilling dive to touch down. St. Helens finished with twelve men after 'Porky' Davies had been sent off, and the Tourists ran out easy winners by 15 - 7.

Britain and France declared war on Germany the next day, in accordance with their pact with Poland. The Kiwi tour was destined to be the shortest in history. They played one more match at Dewsbury and left for home.

144   *Survival of the Fittest (1933 — 1939)*

For the next six years the nations of the Commonwealth joined together in the fight against the common foe. Many Saints players covered themselves in glory of a different kind on the battlefields of the Second World War, and longed for the day when they would be free to play the game they loved once more. Several, like the dashing young scrum-half Harry Briscoe were to make the ultimate sacrifice.

Go to bed Rugby
Just for a while,
Go rub your joints down
With Elliman's — and i'le
P'raps the posts'll split
And the speckers all will flit
But we're going to wake 'em — tomorrow
Bye Bye!

From The St. Helens Lantern — 9th May, 1890

Statistically Speaking

THE SAINTS' PLAYING RECORD 1895-1939
TEAM RECORD
THE HONOURS BOARD

League Champions 1932
Challenge Cup Finalists 1897, 1915, 1930
Lancashire League Winners 1930, 1932
Lancashire Cup Winners 1926. Finalists 1932.
Second Division Runners-up 1903/04
South West Lancs. and Border Towns Cup Winners 1900

THE LEAGUE:

Competition	Season	No. Clubs	Posn	P	W	D	L	F	A	Pts	%
N League	1895/96	22	14	42	15	8	19	195	230	36+	
Lancs. Snr.	1896/97	14	9	26	10	4	12	122	160	24	
Competition	1897/98	14	8	26	10	2	14	161	192	22	
″	1898/99	14	8	26	12	3	11	168	180	27	
″	1899/1900	14	4	26	16	3	7	207	119	35	
″	1900/01	14	13	26	6	2	18	82	228	12*	
″	1901/02	13	3	24	16	1	7	208	114	33	
Division One	1902/03	18	17	34	9	2	23	125	309	20	
Division Two	1903/04	17	2	32	27	1	4	389	57	55	
Division One	1904/05	18	17	34	9	1	24	168	351	19	
N League	1905/06	31	14	30	16	1	13	244	212	33	55
″	1906/07	26	22	26	9	0	17	374	353	18	34.6
″	1907/08	27	25	32	7	3	22	228	500	17	26.6
″	1908/09	31	17	28	11	3	14	312	421	25	44.6
″	1909/10	28	10	31	18	2	11	468	367	38	61.3
″	1910/11	28	19	34	14	1	19	377	449	29	42.6
″	1911/12	27	7	32	21	0	11	527	283	42	65.6
″	1912/13	26	16	32	14	1	17	370	331	29	45.3
″	1913/14	25	19	32	12	1	19	376	440	25	39.1
″	1914/15	25	7	32	19	0	13	368	342	38	59.4
War	1915/16	24	13	26	10	3	13	188	259		44.2
Emergency	1916/17	26	21	23	8	0	15	138	266		34.8
League	1917/18	12	17	18	4	2	12	94	261		27.8
Lancs. League	1918/19	12	11	9	3	0	6	29	109	6	33.3
N League	1919/20	25	16	30	12	2	16	278	285	26	43.3
″	1920/21	25	17	30	14	0	16	254	304	28	46.7
″	1921/22	26	22	34	12	1	21	255	399	25	36.8
″	1922/23	27	19	34	13	0	21	364	427	26	38.2

Statistically Speaking

Competition	Season	No. Clubs	Posn	P	W	D	L	F	A	Pts	%
N League	1923/24	27	16	34	16	0	18	332	522	32	47
"	1924/25	27	10	34	17	3	14	332	381	37	54.4
"	1925/26	27	10	34	18	2	14	410	282	38	55.9
"	1926/27	29	4	34	23	1	10	538	283	47	69.1
"	1927/28	28	11	36	19	1	16	485	336	39	54.2
"	1928/29	28	10	38	19	4	15	460	381	42	55.3
"	1929/30	28	1	40	27	1	12	549	295	55	68.7
"	1930/31	28	7	38	25	1	12	502	344	51	
"	1931/32	28	2	38	29	2	7	699	279	60	
"	1932/33	28	11	38	20	2	16	554	494	42	
"	1933/34	28	13	38	20	0	18	550	500	40	
"	1934/35	28	21	38	14	3	21	278	377	31	
"	1935/36	30	23	38	13	1	24	272	399	27	
"	1936/37	30	22	38	13	4	21	343	431	30	
"	1937/38	29	21	36	14	3	19	370	476	31	
"	1938/39	28	21	40	17	0	23	387	494	34	

+ Two points deducted for ineligible player
* Two points deducted for breach of professional rules

50 points or more — for and against — 1895 to 1939

FOR:
20th March, 1897	v	Lees (H) NU Cup Rd.1 — 58 - 0
20th March, 1907	v	Liverpool City (H) Lge. — 68 - 0
15th February, 1913	v	Coventry (H) Lge. — 51 - 9
21st April, 1923	v	Bradford (H) Lge. — 56 - 10
16th February, 1924	v	Wardley (A) RLC Cup, Rd.1 — 73 - 0
7th October, 1926	v	Pemberton (H) L.Cup Rd.1 — 51 - 8
27th November, 1926	v	York (H) — 54 - 3
16th October, 1933	v	Rochdale (H) — 52 - 14

AGAINST:
12th April, 1909	v	Warrington (A) Lge. — 6 - 78
10th October, 1917	v	Barrow (A) Lge. — 3 - 50
10th April, 1925	v	Wigan (A) Lge. — 4 - 51
3rd April, 1929	v	Hunslet (A) Lge. — 3 - 53

Statistically Speaking 147

THE CHAMPIONSHIP OF ST. HELENS
'Derby' Clashes 1919-1939

Saints and Recs first played each other three times in the temporary Lancashire League of 1918/19:

18.1.18	Knowsley Road	Saints	3	Recs	24
22.3.19	City Road	Saints	0	Recs	18
3.5.19	City Road	Saints	8	Recs	2

The Northern League was resumed in the 1919/20 season.

Date	Venue	Competition	Saints' Score	Recs' Score
25.12.19	City Road	N Rugby League	6	21
1. 1.20	Knowsley Road	"	9	8
25.12.20	"	"	0	5
1. 1.21	City Road	"	0	39
24.12.21	"	"	0	6
31.12.21	Knowsley Road	"	7	6
25.12.22	"	"	2	14
1. 1.23	City Road	"	13	8
25.12.23	"	"	2	21
1. 1.24	Knowsley Road	"	4	0
25.12.24	"	"	7	5
1. 1.25	City Road	"	5	5
25.12.25	"	"	3	3
1. 1.26	Knowsley Road	"	4	2
20.11.26	Warrington	Lancs. Cup Final	10	2
25.12.26	Knowsley Road	N Rugby League	6	6
1. 1.27	City Road	"	8	17
23. 4.27	"	Championship Play-off. S. Final	0	33
24.12.27	"	N Rugby League	2	5
31.12.27	Knowsley Road	"	5	22
25.12.28	"	"	0	5
1. 1.29	City Road	"	2	8
25.12.29	"	"	8	3
1. 1.30	Knowsley Road	"	0	3
8. 2.30	"	R. L. Challenge Cup 1st Round	9	7
25.12.30	"	N Rugby League	7	6
1. 1.31	City Road	"	3	5
25.12.31	"	"	2	13
1. 1.32	Knowsley Road	"	7	7
26.12.32	"	"	8	3
2. 1.33	City Road	"	10	5
2.11.33	"	Lancashire Cup Semi-Final	2	9

Date	Venue	Competition	Saints' Score	Recs' Score
25.12.33	City Road	N Rugby League	9	11
1. 1.34	Knowsley Road	"	10	2
25.12.34	"	"	6	2
1. 1.35	City Road	"	2	2
25. 9.35	Knowsley Road	Lancashire Cup 2nd Round	2	2
30. 9.35	City Road	Lancashire Cup 2nd Round Replay	21	8
25.12.35	"	N Rugby League	3	0
1. 1.36	Knowsley Road	"	5	3
23. 9.36	City Road	Lancashire Cup 2nd Round	4	10
25.12.36	Knowsley Road	N Rugby League	4	0
1. 1.37	City Road	"	3	10
25.12.37	"	"	10	2
1. 1.38	Knowsley Road	"	8	3
26.12.38	"	"	4	5
2. 1.39	City Road	"	5	3

Individual Records

REPRESENTATIVE HONOURS 1895-1939

GREAT BRITAIN

A. Ellaby, L. Fairclough, A. Fildes, A. Frodsham.

ENGLAND

J. Arkwright, T. Barton, A. Ellaby, L. Fairclough, A. Frodsham, J. Garvey, B. Halfpenny, L. Houghton, F. Lee, W. Mercer, F. Tracey.

WALES

I. Davies, O. Griffiths, G. Lewis, F. Roffey.

LANCASHIRE

J. Arkwright, W. Briers, A. Butler, C. Crooks, R. Doherty, A. Ellaby, L. Fairclough, J. Flanagan, T. Foulkes, A. Frodsham, J. Garvey, C. Glover, H. Halsall, S. Hill, L. Houghton, R. Jones, F. Lee, E. McLoughlin, J. Mavitty, W. Mercer, P. Molyneux, J. Prescott, W. Prescott, T. Sudlow, D. Traynor, F. Trenwith, T. Winnard.

CUMBERLAND

W. Ashburner, W. Hillen.

WESTMORELAND

W. Cross, R. Doherty, J. Simpson, J. Thompson, W. Whiteley.

MONMOUTHSHIRE

G. Lewis, F. Roffey.

GLAMORGAN & MONMOUTHSHIRE

E. Dowdall, G. Lewis.

Individual Records

Players appearing in all games in a season

1896/97	W. Briers
1897/98	R. Doherty
1900/01	R. Doherty
	T. Foulkes
1902/03	J. Thompson
1908/09	W. Briers
1909/10	J. Flanagan
	H. Turtill
1911/12	H. Turtill
1913/14	J. Flanagan
1922/23	T. Flynn
1928/29	H. Smith
1931/32	R. Hardgrave

Most Consecutive Appearances

86   H. Smith — October 1927 to October 1929

30 or more tries in a season

50	Alf Ellaby — 1926/27
44	Roy Hardgrave — 1931/32
37	Tom Barton — 1914/15
	Alf Ellaby — 1930/31
34	Roy Hardgrave — 1932/33
33	Alf Ellaby — 1927/28
	Roy Hardgrave — 1929/30
	Alf Ellaby — 1929/30
	Alf Ellaby — 1931/32
32	Roy Hardgrave — 1930/31
31	Jim Flanagan — 1909/10
30	Alf Ellaby — 1928/29
	Roy Hardgrave — 1933/34
	Jim Flanagan — 1910/11

Most goals in a Season

107   George Lewis — 1926/27

Most tries in a match

6   Alf Ellaby   v   Barrow — 5.3.32

Ten or more goals in a match

1922/23	21st April	George Lewis 10	v	Bradford Northern
1923/24	16th February	George Lewis 13	v	Wardley
1928/29	30th March	Ernie Shaw 10	v	Bradford Northern
1931/32	26th September	George Lewis 11	v	Dewsbury

Bibliography

BARKER, T. C. — "Pilkington Brothers and the Glass Industry". Unwin & Allen (1960)

BARKER, T. C., HARRIS J. R. — "A Merseyside Town in the Industrial Revolution". Liverpool (1954)

DALBY, K. — "The Headingley Story 1890-1955".

DAVIES, R. — "Seventy-five Years of Great Britain Rugby League Tours". B.R.L.L.A. (1985)

GAULTON, A. N. — "The Encyclopaedia of Rugby League Football". Hale (1968)

CANON SELWYN GUMMER — "The Chavasse Twins". Hodder & Stoughton (1963)

HODGKINSON, D. — "Heroes of Rugby League". Allen & Unwin (1983)

HOWES, D., FLETCHER, R. (Eds.) — "Rothmans Rugby League Year Books". Rothmans Publications Limited (1981-1985)

MACKLIN, K. — "The History of Rugby League Football". Stanley Paul (1962)

REV. F. MARSHALL (Ed.) — "Football — The Rugby Union Game". Cassell Limited (1892)

MESSENGER, DALLY R. — "The Master — The Story of H. H. 'Dally' Messenger". Angus & Robertson (1982)

MORGAN, J., NICHOLSON, G. — "Report on Rugby". S.B.C., London (1961)

MORRIS, G., HUXLEY, J. — "Wembley Magic". Evans Bros. Limited (1983)

ROBINSON, J., DOVE, F. — "The History of Wigan 1872-1946".

WARING, E. (Ed.) — "The Eddie Waring Book of Rugby League Football". Mueller (1966)

WARING, E. — "Rugby League — The Great Ones". Pelham Books (1969)

ST. HELENS R.L.F.C. — Committee Minute Books. 1904-1939

ST. HELENS R.L.F.C. — Handbooks, 1949, 1955, 1961, 1965

Bibliography

Rugby Leaguer History of Rugby League, Nos. 1-32 Ed. by I. Saxton

Widnes R.F.C. — "Illustrated Cup Final Souvenir". Weekly News (1930)

Widnes R.L.F.C. — Centenary Brochure 1873-1973, Ed. by K. Macklin

Cullet Magazine, Number 95, Spring 1952 — "Early Sports Clubs in St. Helens".

Rugby League Magazine, Volume 1, Number 9 — "The First Tourists from Down-Under". By A. N. Gaulton

Rugby League Magazine, Volume 3, Number 28 — "Let's Reminisce" by D. D. Cross

Rugby League Review, Mid-January, 1949 — Number 21 — "Spotlight on St. Helens" by T. A. Owen

St. Helens Standard (1874)

St. Helens Lantern (1888-1890)

St. Helens Newspaper and Advertiser (1890-1939)

St. Helens Reporter (1890-1939)